POCKET GUIDE TO
SHAMANISM

D1085916

TOM COWAN

BOOK FAITH INDIA
Delhi

POCKET GUIDE TO SHAMANISM

Published by
BOOK FAITH INDIA
414-416 Express Tower
Azadpur Commercial Complex
Delhi, India 110033
Tel. [91-11] 713-2459. Fax [91-11] 724-9674
E-mail: pilgrim@del2.vsnl.net.in

Distributed by
PILGRIMS BOOK HOUSE
P.O.Box 3872
Kathmandu, Nepal
Tel. [977-1] 424942. Fax [977-1] 424943.
E-mail: pilgrims@wlink.com.np
WebSite: www.pilgrimsbooks.com

Varanasi Branch
PILGRIMS BOOK HOUSE
B 27/98-A-8, Durga Kund
Varanasi, India 221001
Tel. [91-542] 314060. Fax [91-542] 314059, 312788
E-mail: pilgrim@lw1.vsnl.net.in

ISBN 81-7303-225-4

Printed in India

Contents

Introduction:
What is Shamanism?

The shaman's path is unending. I am an old, old
man and still a baby, standing before the mystery of
the world, filled with awe.

—don José Matsuwa, a Huichol shaman, in
Shamanic Voices

Shamanism has been part of human culture for tens of thousands of years, so it is no wonder that there is a lot of con-
fusion about what it is—as well as what it has been
throughout the ages and around the world. Prehistoric rock
art found in caves and on cliffs in many parts of the world
suggests that our ancestors were working with shamanic
themes perhaps 40,000 years ago, judging by the wealth of
animal drawings and pictures of humans either dancing or
lying in trance or ecstatic states, wearing bird or animal
masks, and in some mysterious sense interacting with the
power that emanates from the animals.

Shaman is a Siberian word that refers to a particular
kind of spiritual healer found in tribal cultures, but this type
of healer is not limited to Siberia. Shamans are part of
indigenous societies on every continent. Clearly, shamanism
is an integral part of human nature, effectively fulfilling
basic human needs or it would probably not have survived
for so many centuries. The current interest in shamanism is

just one more indication that whatever shamanism is, it is something that enriches human life.

What is shamanism? It is a system of healing based on spiritual practices that originated in tribal cultures. The shaman is a healer who acquires knowledge, wisdom, and spiritual power from personal helping spirits whom the shaman encounters on journeys into other realities. In other words, shamans know and use specific techniques for altering consciousness so that they can access spiritual realities normally invisible and undetectable to people whose conscious awareness is usually focused on the ordinary reality of daily life. The shaman is a "walker between the worlds," able to see and enter realms intentionally that most people encounter only in dreams and myth, and from these realms the shaman brings back vital information for the healing of individuals, the community at large, or the Earth itself.

It is important to distinguish between shamanic techniques of accessing spiritual power and the shaman's services to the community in which he or she lives. What designates a shaman is not the specific activities that he or she performs within the community, but how the shaman derives the knowledge and power to perform those activities. For example, a shaman may prescribe herbal remedies for someone who is ill, but there may well be other herbalists in the community who are not shamans. Or, a shaman may interpret a troubling dream for someone, even though there are other individuals in the village who are also respected dream interpreters.

What distinguishes the shaman's methods? In the case of illness, a shaman would consult with his or her spirit advisers before prescribing herbs, asking, for example, what herbs would be best for an individual. The helping spirits may tell the shaman to prescribe the traditional herbs that everyone in the village agrees is best for a particular illness, or they may instruct the shaman to prescribe something unique for the patient. Also, the shaman may journey into the spirit realms to consult directly with the spirits of the plants before prescribing them. In the case of dream interpretation, a shaman might consult with spirit teachers about the meaning of a dream or journey back into the dream to question the figures who appeared in it to gather understanding about the dream and learn what to tell the dreamer.

In whatever capacity the shaman serves others, knowledge and power come from the spirits who are the shaman's personal instructors and helpers. The typical services that shamans perform include: extraction of harmful intrusions that cause sickness or bad luck, soul retrieval, dream interpretation, divination, exorcism, assistance at births and deaths, and ceremonial work for tribal events and rites of passage.

The spirits who advise and empower shamans are personal to each shaman. They may include traditional deities, such as the gods and goddesses that everyone in the tribe acknowledges, but often include other spirits known only to the shaman. These can be particular animal spirits, such as bear, eagle, mouse, or deer; the spirits of place, such as the spirit of a particular mountain, river, tree, grove, or star; the elemental spirits of air, water, fire, and earth; and ancestral spirits, such as the spirits of deceased members of the village or of the shaman's own family.

The *Pocket Guide to Shamanism* explores the mysteries of shamanism from two points of view: the traditional shaman trained in an indigenous culture, as well as the shamanic practitioner trained in core shamanic practices that are found worldwide. Both traditional shamans and shamanic practitioners are actively engaged in important healing work. From many diverse backgrounds and cultures, they bring visions of the spirit realms that are the true ground of our existence to inspire, encourage, and heal men and women disconnected from their spiritual power and lost in the material realities of contemporary society. As the Huichol shaman Matsuwa reminds us, the path of shamanism is unending, for we are always seeking the meaning of life and standing in awe before the mysteries of the universe.

Chapter One:
Traditional Shamanism

When Western travelers and explorers first encountered shamans in tribal cultures, they did not know what to make of them. Whether viewed from a religious perspective, as was typical in the seventeenth and eighteenth centuries, or from a psychological standpoint, as characterized by the nineteenth and twentieth centuries, the shaman appeared strange and dangerous. From a traditional Christian perspective, shamans dealt with spirits that Christianity did not recognize or consider to be accessible and beneficial to human beings: the spirits of animals, the land, the elements, the dead. Usually the shaman's helping spirits were misinterpreted by Christian observers as "evil spirits" or "demons." When viewed in modern mental-health terms, shamans seemed sick, delusional, or outright crazy. A shaman talks to trees, rocks, and other supposedly "nonintelligent" entities and claims to have magical powers to shapeshift into other forms, to visit invisible realms, and to consort with the dead.

It took several centuries of contact with tribal peoples for Westerners to overcome their misconceptions and appreciate shamans for their healing abilities, insights into human behavior, and role in maintaining harmony within their communities. This chapter explores the calling, training, and world view of traditional shamans, as well as the various services they perform for their communities.

THE CALL TO BECOME A SHAMAN

Americo Yabar, a Q'ero shaman in the Andes, says that to become a shaman "involves a transmission...[that] can come from the lightning, from a master who determines you are ready, or from a feeling inside yourself that you have been called to that path as a vocation. All three paths are strange and difficult." In a nutshell, Yabar calls attention to the three traditional paths to becoming a shaman found in native cultures the world over: a personal life crisis; selection and training by elders; and self-selection by close attention to the spirit within.

Personal Life Crisis

The most dramatic call to being a shaman is the personal life crisis: being struck by lightning, as Yabar puts it. The candidate may develop a life-threatening illness, become severely depressed, suffer a near-death experience, go into a coma for a period of time, or be chronically afflicted by some disease or handicap. In some cultures, what we would call epilepsy, hysteria, and psychotic episodes indicate that the spirits are calling a man or woman to follow the path of shamanism.

The North American Gitskan shaman Isaac Tens relates this type of call. One day while gathering firewood in the hills "a large owl...took hold of me, caught my face, and tried to lift me up. I lost consciousness." When Tens came to, he went down the trail, feeling that the trees had come to life and were pursuing him. He arrived home, told his father what had happened, and then fell into a trance. Shamans were called to help, and when Tens recovered, he felt flies were swarming over his face and that he was drifting in a huge whirlpool. "My heart was thumping fast," he recalled. The shamans told him "that the time had arrived for me to become a *halaait* [shaman] like them."

In traditional native cultures, elder shamans who have gone through the same or similar experiences can help the candidate understand what is occurring, how to get through it, and what it signifies spiritually. In other words, elders put the crisis into a sacred context so that the initiate can understand it from a spiritual perspective. Usually this means helping the shamanic candidate to view the crisis as a call from the spirits, an important and privileged opportunity to see deeper into the mysteries of life and to live in ways more responsive to the spiritual nature of the universe. Overcoming the crisis requires personal healing brought about by the candidate's own efforts, the assistance of elder shamans, and the all-important help of the spirits. When the crisis is resolved, and if the candidate accepts the call to shamanhood, then structured training begins under the tutelage of the elders and the helping spirits.

Although the personal life crisis is the most dramatic and exotic entry into the world of shamanism, it is not the only way. Many shamans are not called so fiercely. Nevertheless, when an individual has embarked on the shaman's path and is in training with elders and helping spirits, there usually occurs a crisis of ego, possibly involving a physical illness, that in some way shatters the neophyte's former sense of security, replacing the older world view with a new way of seeing. The young shaman acquires a stronger sense of the spirit world and develops a commitment to live a more intensely spiritual life. Although other members of the community share the same world view, the shaman has embarked on a deeper, more encompassing intimacy with the spirit world.

Selection by Elders

The second path for becoming a shaman is to be selected by elders, either very early in childhood or at puberty. As in our own culture, adults can recognize a spiritually sensitive child and encourage his or her interest in sacred matters. All children, even in Western culture, begin life with a mystical, intuitive sense of communion with the universe—talking to trees and flowers, "pretending" they are birds and animals, chanting repetitive lyrics and dancing ecstatically, believing in the world of spirits, and investing certain objects, such as blankets, stuffed animals, or dolls, with "magical powers." But only a few children retain this mystical approach to life in later years. A wise parent or teacher can nurture that mysticism and encourage the child to pursue activities that may lead to some sort of professional religious life. The same occurs in indigenous cultures. In some places, shamans use divination to select a young child for shamanic training from among likely candidates. Sometimes shamanic power and practices are passed down from parent to child.

In the 1980s I was privileged to spend time with a Cherokee medicine man in North Carolina whose life followed this path. As a young child he was singled out as someone who would be receptive to learning the traditional ways and was entrusted to his grandfather for intense training in healing and spiritual practices. He spoke Cherokee exclusively, lived more remotely from mainstream society than did his contemporaries, underwent long periods of fasting and isolation, and did not learn English until much later in life.

Among the Manchu people in Mongolia, there are two types of shamans: a selected shaman and a clan shaman. The selected shaman is chosen when the spirit of an ancestral shaman enters a child, who then begins to display supernatural powers or falls ill with a mysterious sickness. The clan shaman is chosen by the clan council or an elder shaman using divinatory techniques. Selected shamans do not need much training by elders for going into trance, journeying to the spirit world, or healing the sick by retrieving lost souls. They do need instruction from elders in performing rituals. Clan shamans, however. need training in all these activities.

Inner Call

Some people know from their earliest days that they are called to lead a more intensely spiritual life than their peers. This inner knowing may come from dreams or from powerful feelings of oneness with the universe, from an abiding sense that helping spirits are present and active in one's life, or from a strong desire to serve the community as a healer or "wise one."

The North American Paviotso shaman Dick Mahwee knew when he was young that he would be a shaman. "When I was a young man, I had dreams in which I doctored people. [But] I did not take those dreams seriously." When he was about fifty, he decided it was time to do something about this, so he went into a cave, where he "prayed and asked for power to doctor sickness." He prayed to the spirit in the cave, the darkness, and then went to sleep and heard "bears, mountain lions, deer, and other animals." He also heard people doctoring and saw a female shaman, then a tall, thin man who gave him a feather and told him to use it in doctoring, along with a deer's hoof, down from an eagle, tobacco, and other objects. "I did as the spirit had ordered and waited to become a doctor. In about six years I had received enough instructions to begin to cure."

Aua, an Eskimo-Iglulik shaman, knew from a prophecy made at his birth that he would grow up to be a shaman. He felt the call from early on, approached elder shamans for training but was refused, grew to manhood, married, had children, and pursued the usual routines of an adult male in his community, all the while hoping against hope that he would someday become a shaman. Then one day he was alone in the wilderness, and there came over him, out of the blue, an overwhelming sense of joy, "a joy so powerful that I could not restrain it...I could see and hear in a totally different way...I was a shaman!"

These two examples illustrate that the call to be a shaman can come early in life, through dreams, personal inclinations, even prophecies from elders. The candidates, however, must act upon them while waiting for the right time, which is not always under the candidate's control. The spirits have their own sense of timing with which the candidate must cooperate.

THE LURE BEYOND ORDINARY REALITY

In all three pathways to shamanhood, the candidate usually feels a strong urge to leave ordinary society and participate more consciously in the nonordinary reality of the spirit world. He or she may become listless, chronically tired, ill, or depressed and prefer to be alone, away from family and friends. In Celtic lands this is known as "being taken by the faeries"; in some cultures it is said that the person is "caught by the spirits." Being caught, called, or taken by the spirits can be experienced as visions or dreams of journeying into the spirit world to meet spirit instructors in the form of power animals or ancestral spirits. Or a candidate might simply become aware of the spirits' presence in his or her own life. At some point the initiate has two choices: to refuse the call or to accept it.

Resisting the call can bring misfortune. Shamans who initially resist the call may remain depressed, sick, unsuccessful in their ordinary lives, and out of sorts with their culture, sometimes for many years. As Uno Harva, a Yakut shaman, put it after years of being a shaman, "Even now I feel unwell and sick whenever I am inactive as a shaman over a longer period of time." For some individuals, only by accepting the call can they recover, feel at home again in ordinary reality, and go on to become shamans.

Not every candidate who resists, however, is subject to misfortune. Dick Mahwee waited until he was about fifty to heed the call that he heard as a young man in his dreams. Jack Stewart, an Owens Valley Paiute, relates, "When I was still a young man, I saw Birch Mountain in a dream." It told him, "You will always be well and strong. Nothing can hurt you and you will live to an old age." But Stewart felt that this work was dangerous and that "sometime in my old age, it would fail me and I would die." He said, "I had another dream…[that said] I should be killed if I were to become a doctor." Throughout his life, he talked to his mountain spirit, and it helped him hunt deer and mountain sheep and guided him in his travels. But he never became a shaman. Stewart lived to a ripe old age.

The life-threatening episodes that may trigger the call or accompany the initial introduction to the presence of spirits in one's life are usually short-lived. The neophyte recovers, healing himself or herself with the spirits' help, and functions remarkably well in society. In fact, the most effective shamans tend to be admired and respected in their communities not just for their shamanic powers, but because they also serve as "ordinary" members performing tasks and filling roles much like everyone else. They hunt, farm, tend their hearths, pursue crafts, and socialize with their families and friends.

TRAINING

Training to be a shaman is a very personal and personalized process. In a sense, elder shamans and helping spirits create a "program" for each shamanic candidate within a traditional framework based on the cultural and spiritual practices of the tribe. In general, training involves asceticism, solitude, and accompanying states of altered consciousness during which the candidate learns what being a shaman will mean in his or her life. By means of extensive and repeated periods of fasting, physical isolation, exposure to the elements, use of psychoactive substances, sensory and sleep deprivation, as well as dreaming, candidates meet and begin relationships with their personal helping spirits. They also assemble sacred tools, costumes, masks, drums, rattles, and other ceremonial objects to use in their shamanic work.

Usually these activities are part of an extended apprenticeship with elder shamans.

Vision Quests

Matsuwa, the Huichol shaman, advises, "To learn to see, to learn to hear, you must do this—go into the wilderness alone...The ways of the gods...are learned only in solitude." Shamans typically have a strong need for periods of isolation from their communities, usually accompanied by fasting, night vigils, and raw exposure to the weather and landscape. Commonly called a vision quest, this kind of experience makes important changes in a person's perception so that the shamanic candidate begins to see and hear in a different way—to see and hear the spirits and journey into their realms. Vision quests are often made at sacred sites or power spots, where Earth energies and spirit activity is unusually strong or perceptible.

Use of Psychoactive Plants

In many indigenous cultures psychoactive substances are used to facilitate visionary experiences. Indigenous people have a deep respect for and relationship with the plants that provide the psychoactive material, viewing them as they do all plants, animals, and natural elements, as conscious, intelligent beings with great power.

Neophytes may be gradually introduced to psychoactive substances over many sessions that slowly build up their knowledge of the plants' effects and their ability to handle them. In fact, an adult will likely have had a gradual and life-long introduction to the plants' effects beginning before birth. If a mother ingests the sacred plants while she is pregnant, the unborn child is affected by them. After birth, the child receives the consciousness-altering substance through the mother's milk. In ceremonies that use psychoactive food or drink, children may be given small doses that they can handle. So by adulthood, an indigenous person may have had considerable experience with the effects of psychoactive plants and have built up a personal response capability that allows for the heavier doses required for shamanic work.

Elders are crucial to helping the shamanic candidate benefit from psychoactive plants. They hunt for the plants and then cut, prepare, and administer them, all of which requires sacred ceremonial activity to honor the plants, which are treated as intelligent, conscious, and powerful beings. Elders also know how to support the candidate while using psychoactive substances and while withdrawing from their influence. Finally, they help the candidate interpret the meaning of the visionary experiences he or she has in the plant-induced altered state of consciousness.

Tests of Spiritual Strength

Elder shamans test a candidate's confidence, resolution, and spiritual strength by assigning seemingly impossible tasks that require great daring, fearlessness, and explicit trust in the spirits. For example, the teacher of Bear Heart, a Muskogee Creek medicine man, required him to walk barefoot through a nest of rattlesnakes while singing his medicine song so that the snakes would make a safe path for him. They did, and then the teacher told Bear Heart to go to the grandfather snake and pat its head. He performed these tasks without any harm but with a good deal of terror.

Dismemberment

Shamanic training often includes a visionary experience in which the neophyte's helping spirits "dismember" his or her body and "doctor" it in some way to cleanse, purify, and strengthen it. Sometimes the spirits replace vital bones and organs with spirit power in the form of crystals, precious stones, sacred herbs or vegetation, metal, or some other power-filled material. The Siberian shaman Kyzlasov reports

> I had been sick and I had been dreaming. In my dreams I had been taken to the ancestors [spirits] and cut into pieces on a black table. They chopped me up and then threw me into the kettle and I was boiled…They found a bone around the ribs which had a hole in the middle…One looks across the hole of this bone and begins to see all, to know all, and that is when one becomes a shaman.

Dismemberment visions may occur repeatedly in a shaman's training, or even later, whenever the spirits feel the shaman needs renewing. It is not uncommon for shamans to see themselves as skeletons in their visions, and it is thought that the prehistoric art found on cave walls and cliffs, depicting skeleton-like people and animals, may derive from these visionary experiences.

Instruction in Tribal Lore

Often a shaman will say that he or she trained for seven, fourteen, or twenty-one years, or even longer. There are several reasons why such extensive training is necessary. First, shamanic power depends on one's relationships with personal spirits who are teachers, guides, and protectors—and it takes time to develop such relationships. The amount of time varies from individual to individual, but getting to know and understand one's spirit guides is the basis of a shaman's power. Equally time-consuming is the memorization of tribal lore regarding sacred stories and herbal remedies.

Since a shaman is a keeper of the folk memory for the tribe, he or she must learn the sacred stories, songs, and chants. In cultures that do not commit sacred information or tribal history to writing, the learning process requires long periods of oral instruction, memorizing, and repeating what is learned. Sometimes songs, chants, and stories must be learned word for word and recited perfectly, such as the Navajo "sings," which go on for several nights.

Herbal knowledge constitutes yet another enormous body of facts and processes that must be transmitted not only orally, but seasonally, if the student is to recognize plants, be able to harvest, prepare, and preserve them, and to know what they are used for. All this may take many years before a shaman feels ready to begin a practice.

Ceremonial Training

A shaman is also a ceremonial leader, which requires hands-on training at ceremonies that may be seasonal or sporadic in the community's life. Although it is true that shamans often receive "customized" instructions for ceremony and ritual from their spirit instructors, they still need to know the traditional ways that ceremonies and celebrations are performed in the tribe.

BECOMING A PRACTICING SHAMAN

A shamanic candidate is ready to begin his or her practice when one or more of the following occurs: another life crisis, a special ceremony arranged by elders and teachers, proof of successful healing, or self-announcement.

After years of training, some candidates undergo another life crisis of some sort that confirms their knowledge and commitment and convinces them that they are ready to practice for others. Sometimes this crisis is orchestrated by the candidate's teachers and elders. It might involve vision questing, fasting, long periods of solitude, tattooing or scarification, and special ceremonial activities to round out the training. Merip Okegei, a Yurok shaman, relates that for two years she repeatedly engaged in a regimen that involved sweat lodge ceremonies every night and drinking no water for ten days at a time. "At such periods I would also gash myself and rub in young fern fronds," she says. Shamans use physical suffering and pain to express their sincerity and commitment and believe that the spirits expect this before they will grant them spiritual power.

As part of the shaman's commitment, the candidate makes vows and accepts personal taboos. These vows and taboos are a kind of contract between the shaman and the spirits, indicating that they will work together for the good of the community. There may also be a formal ceremony in the community to announce publicly that the elders consider the candidate to have finished the training and to be now ready to practice.

In some cultures, shamans may not train for such great lengths of time. In the case of the selected shamans noted among the Manchu of Mongolia, a great clan ritual is held to announce that the individual is indeed a shaman, but since he has already received power and healing abilities from the possessing spirit, he does not need much formal training from elders.

Whether after extensive training or a shorter period of initiation, a shaman may begin practicing publicly and formally by performing a successful healing on someone or accomplishing some other typical shamanic service (see below) that impresses members of the community. In other words, success at shamanic work confers the status of shaman on the individual regardless of formal training. The community's acknowledgment of this is seen by the fact that people start coming to the new shaman for healing and other services.

Lastly, by listening to their helping spirits, shamans often know within themselves that they are ready to proclaim themselves shamans. This may come after long years of training, but in some cases a candidate may have considerable innate shamanic skills and lifelong relationships with personal spirits that speed up the process of realizing his or her shamanic capabilities. Dick Mahwee related that he did what the spirits told him in his dream and then "waited...about six years" to begin curing people. There is really no set length of time to train for shamanhood.

However candidates announce their readiness to function as shamans, the proof is in successful work. As long as a shaman continues to learn, heal, and help others, he or she is a shaman. If shamans fail too often or too consistently, the community will no longer accept them as shamans. It is not uncommon for a shaman to lose powers, helping spirits, and the desire to be a shaman after years of work. This time off may be temporary or permanent.

SHAMANIC SERVICES

Not every shaman performs the same services. It is not unusual for a tribal community to have several or even many shamans specializing in different activities. It is estimated that among the Jívaro of the Amazon about one out of four adult men is a shaman. In some communities, one person in each "extended" family of several generations, including aunts, uncles, and cousins, has shamanic abilities. As with any human skill or talent, nature does not create us all equal. Some shamans are better at some services than at others, either because they have a natural aptitude for them, more extensive training, or spirits that empower them.

Following are the most common shamanic services found in tribal cultures.

Healing the Spirit

The shaman's view of disease is that it is a loss of personal power, or what might be called life force. Commonly this condition is seen as soul loss or a weakening of spirit. Healing therefore involves the restoration of power, life force, or soul, and can be done in several ways.

First, a shaman determines whether a "foreign" spirit or form of energy may have entered the patient because of a "hole" or "gap" in the patient's energy, and if so, proceeds to remove this intrusion. *Extraction* is the technical term for removing harmful energy or spirits and is done in a ceremonial or ritual context. The shaman sucks the extraction out of the body into his or her own mouth and then spits it into water or blows it into some fetish that is then buried, burned, or in some way destroyed. Or the shaman pulls the extraction out by hand and casts it into water or inserts or blows it into a fetish.

The shaman is then ready to restore spiritual power to the patient. This can be done by journeying into the spirit world to bring back some object that contains life force and then either blowing its essence into the patient or presenting it to the patient in some symbolic form, such as a crystal, leaf, feather, or stone. Or the shaman can journey to bring back a spirit helper, such as a power animal, for the patient and then blow it into the patient's head or heart, instructing the patient on how to honor the spirit and use it for protection.

Another method of restoring power to the patient is soul retrieval. In cases where the person's soul has wandered, gotten lost, or been stolen, the shaman journeys into the spirit world to hunt for that soul (or soul part) and bring it back for the patient. The shaman blows the soul or soul part into the patient to restore power.

In each of these cases, the goal is to bring back spiritual power that will "fill up" the patient so that he or she is less susceptible to malignant influences that can cause disease and misfortune.

Herbal Healing

Typically in indigenous cultures shamans have a wide knowledge of herbal remedies, as do many others who are not shamans. Healing often involves prescribing herbs or potions to cure illnesses or alleviate symptoms. As mentioned above, the difference between a shamanic herbalist and a regular herbalist is that the shaman may ask the spirits which herbs would be best for a particular patient. This might include consulting the spirits of the plants themselves.

Bodywork

Shamans may also have skills at working physically on an injured body. The most common techniques are manipulation (similar to chiropractic adjustments), massage, and setting broken bones.

Divination

Divination is the practice of acquiring information about something from "unseen" sources, usually by reading physical signs and omens that occur in nature or that result from a pattern seen in objects that are used as divinatory tools, such as stones, runes, sticks, or cards. Shamans may use divination tools and ask their spirit advisers how to interpret them. Or shamans may journey into the spirit world and ask the spirits directly for the information that is needed. Typical concerns in tribal cultures that may require divination are: locating herds for the hunt; predicting weather; deciding when to move camp; determining auspicious times for ceremonies, sacrifices, or going to war. Individuals also consult shamans for information about their friends and family members, health, love, pregnancy and childbirth, death, and dreams.

Dreamwork

Dream interpretation is a form of divination to help a dreamer understand the meaning of a dream. A shaman consults his or her spirits about the dream's meaning or journeys in spirit into the dream and explores it, questions the figures in it, or possibly changes it to be more auspicious for the dreamer's well-being. Dreams are taken more seriously in native cultures than in our own as vehicles for divine messages, predictions about the future, and instructions for daily life. With the rise of psychotherapy, dreams have found a niche in our culture as vehicles for understanding the self and for restoring mental and emotional health.

Soul-leading

The archaic term *psychopomp* literally means a "conductor or leader of souls." Traditionally, shamans are psychopomps. They assist at births and deaths, both of which are important moments when the barriers between the spirit world and the physical world are lifted to allow souls to enter or leave. Shamans perform rituals, pray, and seek the assistance of spirits to help the souls of the dying leave this world and enter the next, as well as to function as midwives to safeguard the lives of mothers and babies during births. Since shamans journey into the Otherworld routinely and understand the process of walking between the physical and spiritual realms, their knowledge and skills qualify them as psychopomps.

Ceremony and Ritual

Shamans often play key roles in tribal ceremony and ritual. In some cultures shamans function as priests and may indeed be priests, although as Joseph Campbell has pointed out, there is an inherent antagonism between shamans and priests. Shamans work with personal spirits, receive personalized instructions, and are consequently fiercely independent, even erratic, in their behavior and healing practices. Priests, on the other hand, tend to "go by the book," performing ritual and ceremony as it has been done for generations. A new priest or priestess can replace a deceased one without any disruption in the chain of command. Indeed, "chain of command" is an apt description, for the priestly role is highly authoritarian, and priests and priestesses are links in preserving the local orthodoxy. Shamans, however, have their own private visions and understanding of spiritual matters and may deviate from the traditional ways of doing things.

Nevertheless, in some cultures shamans function as priests and ceremonialists, conducting large, public, group activities for the purpose of honoring the gods, assuring good weather or an abundant crop, or offering thanks for a successful hunt or battle. They may also be called to conduct private rituals, such as for a safe birth, an easy death, recovery from illness, safety in the hunt or battle, or protection for the home. Shamans may seek information from helping spirits as to the format, timing, and specific components of a ceremony. They can also give individualized instructions for ritual activities, prayers, and private practices.

THE SHAMAN'S WORLD VIEW

A remarkable consistency exists among indigenous people the world over as to the three-part structure of the cosmos. Often represented as a World Tree, the cosmos consists of three distinct but interpenetrating realms: a lower world existing beneath the surface of the earth and represented by the roots; an upper world existing above the sky and represented by the branches; and a middle world existing on the physical plane where we live our ordinary lives and represented by the trunk.

Shamans journey into these three worlds for knowledge, power, and understanding. There are cultural differences as to the exact nature and geography of these three worlds and the types of spirits and spiritual experiences that can be found in them. The following are generalized descriptions that may or may not be applicable to a given culture in their details, but which taken collectively describe the general features of the three worlds.

The lower world is the realm of Earth energies, animal spirits, the faery folk, and the realm of the dead who have not moved on to the next level of existence. Knowledge of the seasons, weather, animal and plant life, and the deceased can be found in the lower world, as well as healing techniques for illness and disease.

The upper world is the realm of heavenly, noncorporeal energies, angelic beings, the spirits who compose the pantheons of gods and goddesses, and the spirits of the deceased who have progressed beyond the land of the dead. Shamans journey to the upper worlds for divine inspiration, knowledge of the "greater universe" (beyond Earth and its galaxy), and to explore parallel universes. Whereas the knowledge and help from lower world spirits tend to be useful for earthly life, knowledge and help from the upper world provide instruction for our roles as spiritual beings who participate in a larger, more cosmic existence.

The middle world comprises essentially the earthly realms of the planet as well as the outer reaches of the universe. Journeys to the middle world can show the shaman actual conditions in ordinary reality or their spiritual aspects. Shamans might journey through the middle world to discover the location of herds, influence weather, or view people and events at a distance. They might also journey to meet land spirits or the spirits of a place, such as a grove of trees or waterfall. Ritual and ceremony to honor or propitiate nature spirits are performed in the middle world.

In some cultures these three realms may be further divided into other levels and sublevels. Individual shamans may also visit private places within the three-part cosmos known only to them, personal power spots in the invisible realms where they go for their own instruction, rest, or healing.

There is also a sense in which the three realms are the same place, or are interconnected and overlapping. It is possible, for example, to journey into the lower world and from there proceed into the upper world. The African !Kung shaman K"xau describes the following:

> I enter the earth. I go in at a place like a place where people drink water. I travel in a long way, very far. When I emerge, I am already climbing. I'm climbing threads, the threads that lie over there in the South...I climb one and leave it, then I go climb another one....Then I leave it and climb on

> another...Then I follow the thread of the wells, the
> one I am going to go enter.

By this time it is difficult to say in which world K"xau is operating, but it really doesn't matter. The shamanic journey takes place in another reality that need not conform to the geography and physics of ordinary reality.

Nor are spirits necessarily confined to one or another realm; angelic spirits can be met in the lower world, and animal spirits in the upper world. Although this may sound contradictory and inconsistent, keep in mind that the geography of the Otherworld is outside space and time as we know them. The spirit world may be thought of as a shapeshifting state of consciousness that responds to the needs of the individual shaman. Our conceptions of physical place and earthly time correspond only roughly to our experiences in nonordinary reality. This is not to say that the Otherworld has no structure or substance, but that it is more like the substance and structure of dreams: magical, shifting, surprising, and embued with many meanings.

RETAINING SHAMANIC POWERS

Sometimes traditional shamans will talk about losing their power or being abandoned by their spirit helpers. They may stop shamanizing for a while, or for the rest of their lives. Why is this?

The spirits who work with human beings have their own personal needs and purposes for doing so which we may never completely comprehend. In most cultures, however, there is an understanding that being a shaman is a mutual enterprise between a human being and his or her specific helping spirits. It is possible that the spirits' need to work with the shaman can come to an end, and so they leave. In such cases, a shaman may be able to meet other helping spirits and continue to practice. But if not, the shaman loses the power to be an effective shaman.

There is also a rather widespread notion that a shaman who uses spiritual power for selfish or harmful purposes will soon lose that power. A common belief found in many cultures is that the harm a shaman does will return threefold and harm the shaman in ways that might result in a loss of power. This does not mean there are no dangerous shamans, but that a shaman who traffics in baneful magic or harmful spells against others (often rival shamans!) is treading in dangerous waters.

Many shamans speak of the need to be humble and to beseech the spirits to take pity on them in their work. At the heart of shamanism is the dependence on spiritual help from other realms and the understanding that we are not alone and cannot perform miracles alone. The shaman is seen by spirit helpers as a compassionate, humble servant dedicated to making life better for others. That is why the spirits take pity on the shaman and work with him or her, and ultimately is why the shaman is effective in healing illness, performing ceremony, divining for necessary information, and ensuring the welfare of the community. A shaman who boasts excessively, takes full credit for his or her powers, or develops an oversized ego with which the spirits refuse to work will soon be abandoned by the spirits and lose shamanic power.

In many parts of the world, shamans talk about losing their powers because of too much contact with Western civilization and Christianity. Some shamans report that when they converted to Christianity or became too involved with Western explorers and developers their helping spirits left them or, in some cases, the shamans had to ask their spirits to go back to the spirit world. Alualuk, an Arctic shaman, sent his helping spirits away when he was baptized a Christian, after which he claimed to be as helpless as other men and women, feeling lonely, weak, and sad. The spirits told him that they missed him too. An Eskimo shaman who also felt abandoned after becoming a Christian said, "Since then they [my helping spirits] have not shown themselves to me because I betrayed them by my baptism."

There is not, however, an inevitable animosity between mainstream religions such as Christianity and private shamanic spiritual experiences. Shamans born into a culture already Christianized may include Jesus, Mary, and other saints and angels among their helping spirits. Eduardo Calderón, a contemporary Peruvian shaman salutes

> the ancients, the powerful ones, ...who have lived in antiquity...*curanderos* who have died and who are alive, calling their spirits, their personalities....I also call on Saint Augustine, Moses, Solomon, Saint Cyprian, Saint Paul, for advice, for help in moments of doubt."

In Asia there is a blending of Buddhism and shamanism. Mongolian shamans, for example, have headdresses that incorporate bird symbolism along with images of the five "meditation Buddhas" of Tibetan Buddhism. Larry Peters, ethnologist and field associate for the Foundation for Shamanic Studies, sees no conflict or antagonism between shamanic belief and practice and Buddhist religion in Mongolia. Says Peters, "They serve distinct and complementary roles, are utilized by each other and…may be combined in one person."

This brief overview of traditional shamanism makes clear that there are various paths to becoming a shaman and various ways to practice shamanism in an indigenous culture. The one great truth of shamanism is that it is a highly personal path, a spiritual life based on intimate relationships with helping spirits and journeys to realms of mystery and power that may be known only to the shaman who goes there. Black Elk, the famous holy man of the Oglala Sioux, put it this way in a prayer to the Creator:

> To the center of the world you have taken me and showed me the goodness and the beauty and the strangeness of the greening earth, the only mother—and there the spirit shapes of things, as they should be, you have shown to me, and I have seen.

In a sense this is the core experience and vision of every shaman. What a shaman does with this knowledge of the "spirit shapes of things" is up to each individual shaman.

Chapter Two:
Modern Shamanism

Modern shamanism, or what some people call neo-shamanism, is based on the core shamanic principles and practices found in indigenous cultures all over the world. Although the setting in which traditional shamans practice is very specific—the natural features of the surrounding landscape, the religious beliefs of their people, the presence of specific animals, the social customs that evolved over generations—the rudimentary beliefs and practices of shamans are remarkably consistent and universal. It has been one of the exciting discoveries in the last twenty or thirty years that Westerners, even those living in major cities, can successfully practice the core elements of shamanism.

CORE SHAMANISM

Core shamanism is a form of shamanism that is based on the common principles and practices found in many indigenous cultures that can be successfully employed in non-indigenous settings. Many practitioners of core shamanism adapt universal or near-universal practices from the world's shamanic lore, rather than restrict themselves to a particular culture's expression of those practices.

The core principles of shamanism are:

- that human beings are able to work productively in altered states of consciousness, which can be induced by monotonous sounds, such as steady drumming or chanting,

- that we can enter other realities normally imperceptible to people who are not working in an altered state of consciousness,
- and that we can bring back from those realities helpful, healing knowledge for ourselves and others.

In traditional shamanic terms, the shaman journeys into the upper or lower worlds to interact with power animals or guardian spirits in order to receive instruction, advice, or information that will be conducive to healing, understanding, decisionmaking, and other everyday issues. This is what shamans do in indigenous cultures, and it is what shamanic practitioners do in our own.

Since roughly the 1960s, teachers of core shamanic practices have introduced shamanism to people whose lifestyles are quite alien to the hunting-gathering-fishing cultures where shamanism originated tens of thousands of years ago. On first glance, it would seem that shamanism would not work outside its ancient setting. But the results have been surprising and dramatic. The successful work of shamanic practitioners—who may be lawyers, social workers, accountants, teachers, truck drivers, computer analysts, psychotherapists—has proven that shamanism is based on a human ability and serves basic human needs irrespective of culture, continent, or century. Although shamanism may seem exotic and rare to individuals whose world views center primarily on contemporary Western civilization, it is not.

On a 1993 trip to Siberia, where the word *shaman* originated, a dozen shamanic practitioners from North America and Western Europe met with indigenous shamans in the Republic of Tuva, and both groups understood each other, worked together shamanically, and performed healing rituals for each other. The trip to Tuva, arranged through the Tuvinian government and the Foundation for Shamanic Studies, confirmed that core shamanic practices learned in a culturally neutral context and the traditional practices rooted in specific indigenous cultures can be equally effective in healing.

The basic practices of core shamanism are:

- the altering of consciousness to produce the "shamanic state of consciousness," a phrase coined by Michael Harner, founder and director of the Foundation for Shamanic Studies,
- the journey into a nonordinary reality that is similar to the reality found in dreams and myths,
- the development of ongoing relationships with helping spirits, including the spirits of animals, the elements, the land, the dead, or the deities and sacred beings of an established religion,
- the healing practices of extraction, power restoration, soul retrieval, and ritual,
- the use of song, dance, costume, and ritual to provide a sacred setting in which to do shamanic work, and
- the valuing of special objects and natural sites that are conducive to a practitioner's personal understanding of shamanic work.

These, along with other secondary and optional practices, are the core activities that both shamans and shamanic practitioners engage in for the same purpose: the seeking of spiritual power in the form of healing, knowledge, and understanding.

THE SHAMANIC REVIVAL

Although shamanism has never died out, many indigenous societies that provided a home for shamanism have disappeared or have been so drastically transformed by modern thought and culture that they no longer nurture shamans. Some native cultures currently have only one or two elderly shamans with no younger apprentices. When these shamans die, ancient shamanic wisdom will die with them. But in addition to being a body of knowledge, shamanism is also a practice based on an innate human ability and serving innate human needs. In this sense, it will never die out completely, and today we are witnessing the reawakening of that ability in people the world over. A 1995 expedition of shamanic practitioners to northeastern China organized by the Foundation for Shamanic Studies found that even in a Communist country where ruthless efforts are made to eliminate religion and "primitive superstitions," shamanism is enjoying a slow but gradual renaissance. How can the remarkable endurance and resiliency of shamanism be explained?

Shamanism as a system of healing and as a spiritual practice satisfies needs that have become urgent in recent years. As people surrender so much of their lives—both physical and psychic—to large institutions, corporations, and sprawling urban areas, there is a growing need to nurture and honor personal dreams, hopes, and visions. Shamanic practices do just that, for the shamanic journey is an ideal vehicle for discovering the personal visionary experiences that allow us to grow and develop as spiritual beings. As pressure builds in society to conform to trends, fads, and the currently "correct" lines of thought, shamanism nurtures diversity by honoring practitioners' personal visions and truths.

The Earth and its communities of life (which include human beings) are desperately crying out for respectful, even worshipful, spiritual practices that honor the planet and all living things. Traditional shamanism comes from animistic cultures where people respected the living spirit within all created things and honored the Earth as the source of life. Shamanic practitioners, no matter what religions they were raised in or continue to practice, find this animistic perspective enriching for their lives, their work, their relationships, even for their primary religious experience. The increasing concern for ecological health, the proper stewardship of natural resources, the diversity of species, and the survival of life as we know it on the planet is fueling interest in shamanic truths and values.

Because shamanism is a personal, even private spiritual practice, it focuses attention on our daily lives—the work, people, places, joys, and sorrows that make up our existence. Unlike mainstream religious customs, which are often centered primarily around churches, synagogues, and temples, large communities of believers, and written dogmas, shamanism is centered on home, family, Earth, and the personal experiences that make up everyday life. It is a spiritual practice rooted where we "live and move and have our being," not where we go to worship on certain days of the week.

Shamanic practitioners also indicate that shamanism awakens some deep, hidden memory or lost knowledge of times past. It honors ancient knowledge and stirs in us the echoes of an older wisdom perhaps long forgotten or buried beneath modern ways of living and thinking. Specifically, people have said that when they first sat on the floor beside a candle or on the ground beside a fire and began to drum or shake a rattle, they felt they were doing something they "didn't know they knew." They felt they had come home. It's possible that such feelings arise deep from within the unconscious, because for most of the millennia that human beings have been alive on this planet, we have lived in small tribal or village cultures close to nature and the spirits of nature. It is only in the last several hundred years that we have lived in densely populated areas separated from animals and organic life. Shamanic rituals awaken in us lost memories and hidden knowledge, still linked to the ancestral wisdom of our forebears.

THE CALL TO BECOME A SHAMANIC PRACTITIONER

Contemporary men and women may be called to the shamanic path by means of a life-threatening or emotionally wrenching crisis, much like traditional shamans. Sometimes the crisis occurs in childhood or adolescence, long before the individual knows about shamanism, and of course without shamanic elders available to explain its significance. The period of suffering, disorientation, and feeling out of sorts with ordinary reality may persist for many years. Sometimes therapy helps alleviate the problem. Later, when the individual discovers shamanism, the crisis can be put into a setting that makes sense in terms of a call to a spiritual lifestyle different from that of mainstream religions. Since shamanism has become more widely understood in our culture, some individuals are already familiar with it when a life crisis occurs, and they turn to shamans or shamanic practitioners for help.

The selection by elder shamans seldom occurs in our society since we don't have many shamanic elders at present. As more and more people become shamanic practitioners, however, they will recognize spiritual interests in their children or the children they work with and, through teaching or by the example of their lives, can encourage spiritually sensitive young people to investigate shamanism. For many practitioners, lectures, workshops, and books were the "elders" that introduced them to shamanism.

A large number of adult practitioners report having felt the inner call to a spiritual path early on; they say they were spiritually sensitive and inquisitive children and have been on a spiritual quest most of their lives. In fact, many practitioners, when asked how they discovered shamanism, will give a two-part answer. They will say they met a shaman, read a book on shamanism, or enrolled in a shamanic training program so many months or years ago, but then will say that what they learned "rang a bell" with experiences they remember from childhood. What were the shamanic experiences of childhood? Talking with invisible friends, hiding in favorite "power spots," playing with toys or objects that had magical significance, singing nonsense rhymes over and over in a kind of mesmerizing chant, and so forth. In other words, people instinctively recognize the elements of the natural mysticism of childhood in the shamanic practices they learn as adults.

Many practitioners have left the religious traditions in which they were raised. They often say they were searching for deeper spiritual truths and experiences than those found in mainstream religions and began investigating alternative spiritual paths, which led to shamanism. But not all people sever their former religious affiliations; some find that shamanism enhances the best beliefs and practices of the religions in which they were reared.

TRAINING

There are various ways to become a shamanic practitioner. Some are parallel to those described in the previous chapter for indigenous shamans. Others are unique to learning shamanism in a nontribal environment.

Teachers

Some Westerners are fortunate to meet native shamans who are willing to accept them as apprentices and train them in the traditional ways of their ancestors. Often this means radically changing one's lifestyle, even moving to live close to teachers, which might mean near the area where the shaman's people live. It may mean learning tribal language, stories, social mores, native plants, and so forth in order to practice shamanism in the traditional way. Few Westerners are willing, or lucky enough, to be trained so thoroughly and to change their way of living to accommodate indigenous shamanic practices and become shamans in this manner. Many simply learn some of the traditional practices and incorporate them into their shamanic work.

Fortunately, there is a growing number of core shamanic instructors who teach the basic core practices, sometimes in conjunction with specific native practices into which they have been initiated. (See Chapter Five for a discussion of the issues involved in borrowing native customs for core shamanic work.) Many contemporary practitioners have studied and trained with these teachers, sometimes for many years. Training may have consisted of a series of weekend workshops or week-long or month-long intensive sessions, all of which might extend over a period of several years. Not only do practitioners learn shamanism from their teachers, but by studying and training with the same group of students over an extended period of time, much learning occurs through mutual sharing of personal experiences.

Most importantly, each shaman and practitioner of shamanism learns from his or her helping spirits. Whether they be power animals, the spirits of deceased shamans or relatives, the spirits of the land and the elements, angelic beings, or the saints and deities of the mainstream religious traditions, teachers in nonordinary reality are the *primary* instructors for anyone serious about practicing shamanism or becoming a shaman. Only by regular journeys into the spirit world and intensive "sessions" with his or her helping spirits does the shamanic student acquire the knowledge and skills to be an effective practitioner.

Publications and Videos

The last few decades have witnessed an enormous explosion in published works by and about shamans. Some of these are written by native shamans, apprentices to native shamans, practitioners who have met indigenous teachers and studied with them, and shamanic practitioners who have pioneered ways to adapt ancient practices to the modern world. Some of these publications are very personal accounts; some are handbooks. While it is not possible to become a shaman or even a shamanic practitioner by reading alone, the growing volume of books and videos on shamanism is a valuable resource for people interested in learning and practicing shamanism (see "Bibliography").

Life Experiences

The specific experiences that are used to train an indigenous candidate for shamanism are also part of the training of shamanic practitioners, with some important differences required by our Western culture, values, attitudes, and previous preparation. Following are some of them.

Teachers of core shamanism provide experiences that introduce students to the way the spirits function in both ordinary and nonordinary realities. Like indigenous elders, teachers determine a sequence of visionary experiences that initiate candidates into the workings of the spirit world. Many of these initiatory experiences are similar to those of tribal cultures. For example, spending extended periods alone in nature, fasting, monitoring one's dreams, chanting and dancing to honor the spirits, and making the shamanic journey a regular spiritual practice—these are activities that prepare a person to be a shamanic practitioner.

Certain adjustments, however, are sometimes necessary to accommodate the urban sensibilities and physical conditions of mainstream people. For example, many Westerners are not physically able to spend time alone in the wilderness on vision quests without special training and preparation. The basic survival skills and wilderness "smarts" that indigenous people pick up spontaneously are new and unfamiliar to most urbanites. City-dwellers may also not have the physical stamina for the rigorous wilderness experiences of tribal people. In a sense, a vision quest is a more exotic experience for a city-dweller than it would be for an indigenous person used to living close to nature. This is not to say that vision quests and night vigils alone in the wilds are not appropriate for shamanic practitioners. They are, but they may have to be conducted in ways that will take into account the person's urban background.

Fasting may also have to be undertaken gradually, since many people in our affluent society are not used to fasting for extended periods of time. In indigenous cultures where food scarcity is a common occurrence, especially during the winter months, everyone learns how to function on reduced nourishment. Fasting is a survival skill.

The use of psychoactive substances to open the doors of perception to the Otherworld presents a dilemma for Westerners. The sensitive relationship that indigenous people have with the plants that grow in their environment is greatly lacking in our culture. Nor do we have elders who can provide a safe procedure and setting for using psychoactive substances. Furthermore, our consumer culture encourages us to view psychoactive plants as "drugs"—that is, products we can buy and put in our bodies for a quick fix, in this case a quick vision of nonordinary realities. Psychoactive substances are spirit teachers, not commercial products. Given our lack of experience with the spiritual realities of nature and our counter-productive attitudes and values rooted in materialism and consumerism, it is doubtful that we can use plants for visionary experiences without a great deal of education, training, and personal supervision. Even when so-called ayahuasca workshops are available and facilitated by visiting shamans from cultures that use ayahuasca (an hallucinogenic plant found in the Amazon Valley), they can be disappointing and even dangerous for Western participants who are not carefully prepared for them. Furthermore, hallucinogens are illegal in the United States, and users risk imprisonment and fines.

BEGINNING A SHAMANIC PRACTICE

If a person is being trained by a native shaman, that shaman will most likely let the candidate know when he or she is ready to begin practicing for others. Some core shamanic training programs have an established "course" of knowledge and practices that candidates must complete before they can present themselves as trained in that program. Having finished a course of instruction, however, does not necessarily make someone an effective shamanic practitioner, just as having a medical degree from a university does not mean that a person can practice medicine legally or even effectively. Having completed a course of instruction means that a person has been exposed to a certain body of knowledge and practices and presumably knows about it intellectually. But much more goes into being a shamanic practitioner than intellectual knowledge. Talents, skills, judgment, and ongoing relationships with helping spirits are also essential to establishing a person as a shamanic practitioner.

The best indication that a candidate is ready to begin practicing is a growing self-confidence, constantly tempered by humility and a fierce dedication to honesty, as well as the approval and encouragement from helping spirits. As with traditional shamans, only successful healing, divination, and ritual work "prove" that an individual has shamanic skills and powers.

ADAPTING SHAMANISM TO WESTERN BELIEF SYSTEMS

In general, shamanic practitioners subscribe to the three-part cosmology of traditional shamans: the spirit world consists of upper, lower, and middle regions. But many practitioners blend into their practice some elements of mainstream religions, concepts derived from Western philosophy and psychology, and both modern and alternative theories of healing. Here are some of the areas in which traditional and more contemporary concepts can be found.

Religion

Indigenous people do not have words in their languages for "religion." When Westerners discovered this, they mistakenly supposed that "primitive" people did not have religions or spiritualities or even knowledge of a Supreme Being or Creator. Instead, they were thought to worship idols and "false gods" and to organize their lives around superstitions and irrational taboos. On the contrary, native people's concept of the sacred is so intimately interwoven in nature, human activity, and in each man's and woman's daily life that the spiritual and the material are inseparable. Rather than not knowing the Creator, native people recognize the Creator and the Creator's power and energy—or Spirit of the Universe—in the smallest pebble, ant, or drop of water, as well as in the great mountains, sky, and stars. The Divine Spirit is everywhere.

Westerners, however, with a considerably narrower view of the sacred (usually dividing experiences into the "sacred" and the "profane," with the majority falling into the latter category) and with a very restricted notion of religion and religious experience, could not recognize as sacred the diversity of beliefs and practices found among indigenous peoples. Westerners also found it—and continue to find it—hard to understand how a spiritual practice or healing technique that is rooted in one's understanding of spirits and the sacred qualities of the universe can thrive independently of orthodox religious structures based on hierarchical institutions. In other words, it is hard for Westerners to understand that shamanism is a spiritual practice and a method of spiritual healing that is not dependent upon any culture's "official religion."

Perhaps an example of a spiritual practice such as fasting will help. Fasting is a practice found in many religious traditions and can be engaged in for different reasons based on the religious beliefs one brings to the fast. For example, you might fast because you view the body as weak or sinful, and fasting as a way of punishing the body. Or, you might fast to identify yourself and your suffering with the hungry people of the world, hoping that your suffering will in some way alleviate or redeem theirs. Or, you may engage in fasting because it alters your consciousness, making you more aware of spiritual activity within you, the presence of spirits around you, or the spiritual insights that can arise in an altered state of consciousness. You might also fast for non-spiritual reasons, such as for physical health.

The same case can be made for pilgrimages, night vigils, vision quests, sweat lodges, prayer, and other spiritual practices that transcend any one religious tradition. Shamanism is a spiritual path that incorporates these practices, along with others that are unique to shamanism, such as the shamanic journey. It is not a religion in itself. About the only spiritual belief that is common to all practitioners is the belief in spirits. Followers of mainstream religions are able to incorporate shamanism into their spiritual lives, just as they can incorporate yoga and zen meditation. Often among their helping spirits are the saints, deities, and divine beings from their primary religion. Shamanic practitioners include people from all religious traditions: Jews, Protestants, Catholics, Buddhists. Even nuns, monks, and clergy from these traditions can practice shamanism successfully and find no conflict with their religious beliefs. Surprisingly, even agnostics and atheists can be shamanic practitioners if they have a flexible view of consciousness, the personal and collective unconscious, and the imaginal realm of the psyche.

Philosophy and Psychology

Some shamanic practitioners routinely use the term *consciousness* instead of *spirit*. Consciousness is a relatively modern term. It began to be used regularly in English during the seventeenth century, usually to refer to a body of knowledge or the totality of thoughts on a subject. In the nineteenth century the idea of a *state* of consciousness emerged in the field of psychology to mean the totality of a person's thinking, feeling, and sensing at any given moment. The term *consciousness* is generally used today to refer to that part of our being that shamans would have called spirit. Ancient shamans did not have the word *consciousness*. They would have said that trees, rocks, rivers, and animals have spirits, whereas modern practitioners might say that these things have consciousness.

Some shamanic practitioners prefer to use the term *consciousness* to refer to their own spirits, or that part of themselves that journeys into the Otherworld. The Otherworld is seen as another state of consciousness, a nonordinary state of consciousness. The altered, nonordinary state of consciousness becomes both the doorway to the invisible realms and the invisible realms themselves.

Shamanic practitioners often borrow concepts from other spiritual systems, psychologies, and so-called New Age thinking in order to explain shamanism to themselves or others. For example, they may refer to their power animals and spirit teachers as aspects of their "higher selves." Or they may consider helping spirits to be Jungian archetypes. A lower-world journey could be viewed as contacting the "personal unconscious" or the "collective unconscious" or an excursion into a "parallel universe." The shamanic state of consciousness itself may be viewed as a kind of "alpha state" based on the brain waves that occur while a person is listening to shamanic drumming.

Modernizing the core concepts of shamanism, however, is not necessary for shamanic practice, but it satisfies many practitioners' need to put their practice into contemporary terms and may help them to explain it to disapproving or skeptical critics. Ultimately, however, modern terms and theories are not necessary for shamanic practice. Shamanism is not theoretical, but empirical. It is not something practitioners have to explain, but something practitioners do and then describe.

Health and Healing

Most shamanic practitioners adopt, to some extent, the traditional shaman's view of disease as a loss of spiritual power. Similarly, they see healing as the restoration of that power. But in both theory and practice, many practitioners incorporate other Western concepts of disease since they are working in a Western setting and with clients and patients who believe in and want Western medicine and technology.

Tribal shamans themselves do not totally shun Western medical practices. Some go to Western-trained doctors, nurses, medical clinics, and pharmacies. But in shamanic thinking, modern medicine alone cannot restore the patient to full living, full consciousness, or full spiritual power. Similarly, shamanic practitioners may rely on Western medicine for its ability to repair the physical body and alleviate symptoms, but most develop a holistic approach to healing, often making a distinction between "curing the disease" and "healing the person." Western remedies notoriously overlook the total person, in favor of eliminating the disease. The "recovered" patient, however, might still feel disabled, guilty, worried, less whole, and fearful of relapses, all of which Western medicine does not address. Shamanism can fill these gaps by addressing the patient's spiritual needs, which include, but extend beyond, the physical and emotional.

For some shamanic practitioners, spiritual needs equate roughly with psychological needs. (The term *psychology* literally means "soul knowledge," even though a great number of psychologists do not perceive their work as dealing with the "soul" in the traditional sense of that term.) A great many shamanic practitioners are, in fact, psychologists by profession and incorporate shamanic practices into their sessions, sometimes using their own skills as shamanic practitioners to do healing work on their clients, and sometimes teaching clients how to practice shamanism. This kind of blending of shamanism and psychotherapy aims to restore clients to fuller, more rewarding, and healthier lives.

Like traditional shamans, shamanic practitioners incorporate ritual into their healing work, believing that it touches deeply upon a person's inner being and facilitates healing. Shamanism restores sacred ritual to our lives, bringing us closer to the natural rhythms of birth, growth, decline, and death, and the spiritual significance of these events in our lives. Shamanic practitioners can provide rituals based on ancient world views that transcend contemporary society, rituals rooted in timeless practices, events, and understandings of nature that help to elevate patients out of depression and illness.

EMBELLISHING THE CORE SHAMANIC PRACTICE

It has been said somewhat facetiously that you can learn core shamanism, but you can't practice it. What is usually implied by this tricksterish statement is that the core shamanic practices cannot be "orphaned" so to be speak from *all* cultural settings. There is a strong urge in practitioners to bring their practice to life with symbol, myth, ritual, landscape, costume, song, and other features of the world's cultures. But how do you go about it? How, for example, do you decide what symbols to paint on your drum, what shamanic clothing, if any, to wear, what songs and chants to sing, where in nature to go for vision quests or night vigils or sacred stones and holy water, and what cleansing and purifying methods to incorporate into your practice?

One solution to these questions—and one that many practitioners employ, particularly in North America—is to "borrow" concepts and practices from Native American traditions. There are serious problems with this approach, and Chapter Five will address this issue in greater depth. For now, I will simply note that taking spiritual and religious practices from other cultures can be a form of religious imperialism or outright stealing. Other cultures' spiritual practices are sacred and should not be engaged in by people who are not trained or initiated into those cultures. Some practices depend on specific theological and social settings to be effective, and many require specific belief systems and ecological settings. And yet there are spiritual practices, like the core shamanic practices, that transcend any particular culture, and no one people has a monopoly on them. Vision quests, fasting, pilgrimages, prayer, use of drums and rattles, and so forth are cross-cultural, and it should not offend any group to learn that other people also engage in them.

Sometimes a practitioner who has studied with an indigenous shaman or elder will pick up practices from the teacher's culture and use them in his or her practice. The practitioner may have been given permission, for example, to smoke a sacred pipe (without being designated an official pipe carrier) or to pour water in a sweat ceremony according to a particular tradition. A practitioner may have been given an eagle feather by a native shaman to use in smudging.

Shamanic practitioners do not need to draw on native customs of North America. There has been a recent revival of old European shamanic practices. Celtic, Norse, Saxon, Sami, and Mediterranean shamanic practices are being rediscovered, revived, and adapted to core shamanic practices. In fact, the core shamanic journey to seek ancestral wisdom is a method for recovering lost shamanic knowledge and practices. Many practitioners of European background and heritage feel more comfortable with this than borrowing native practices from traditions to which they know they will never belong.

The practice of core shamanism in its many styles and manifestations is a vital part of the resurgence in the Earth-oriented, "green" values and attitudes that are shaping our efforts to live more sensitively and respectfully with the planet. In whatever walks of life we find shamanic practitioners, we meet men and women striving to refocus their lives in the broader contexts of landscape and spirit.

Chapter Three:
Varieties of Shamanic Healing

The Lakota visionary Lame Deer once said, "If all was told—supposing there lived a person who could tell all—there would be no mysteries left, and that would be very bad. Man cannot live without mystery. He has a great need of it." Men and women of every age have sought ways to participate intelligently and soulfully in the mysteries of life. In the brief years we live on the Earth, we hunger for understanding and strive to heal our suffering. Shamanism is one way to do this for it engages the mind, heart, and soul with the wonders of creation wherein we find the source of healing and understanding. But shamanism is just a beginning. It does not answer all our questions, nor should it. Lame Deer's observation is a sound one. Malidoma Somé, a Dagara shaman from West Africa, concurs, "The Dagara refrains from asking questions when faced with a riddle because questioning and being answered destroys one's chance to learn for oneself. Questions are the mind's way of trying to destroy a mystery." And we do not want to destroy the mystery, for ultimately, the mysteries of life are the mysteries of the human soul.

This chapter explores the specific ways that various shamans and shamanic practitioners approach these mysteries. The sampling of individuals in this chapter is a personal one, selected to present the rich variety of shamanic activity and to introduce readers to some of the applications of shamanism, which, like shamanism itself, transcend continents, centuries, and cultures.

A HEALING VISION FOR A PEOPLE

At the heart of shamanism is the personal visionary life of the shaman. The personal vision encompasses the friendship of spirit helpers and the great invisible realms that lie above, below, and beside our world of ordinary reality. In various ways shamans mine their visions of nonordinary realities for useful and inspiring knowledge, methods of healing, and ways to be of service to their communities. For some shamans the initiatory vision comes spontaneously during a life crisis.

Black Elk, the great Lakota holy man, was called to be a spiritual leader for his people during a childhood illness. Born in 1863, Black Elk witnessed and lived through the years in which Native Americans lost their remaining land west of the Mississippi River and found their lives continually disrupted by U.S. Government policies of intimidation, coercion, and vacillation. Black Elk's boyhood vision was a preface to these disasters.

Black Elk fell sick quite suddenly when he was nine years old. His legs, arms, and face swelled up; he couldn't walk. While he lay in his teepee, he saw two men coming down from the clouds who took him up through the sky, where he saw twelve black horses in the west, twelve white horses in the north, twelve sorrel horses in the east, and twelve buckskin horses in the south. The horses were dancing. Then he was taken to the Grandfathers, the Ancient Ones, who predicted that the boy would be a healer for his people. They showed him the Earth, which he saw "lying yonder like a hoop of peoples, and in the center bloomed the holy stick that was a tree." He learned that all the birds, the winds, and the stars would be his spirit helpers, who would alleviate the sickness of the Earth and his people. The Grandfathers gave him power objects: "the cup of water and the bow and arrows, the power to make live and to destroy; the white wing of cleansing and the healing herb; the sacred pipe; the flowering stick."

Black Elk described his vision in this way: "While I stood there I saw more than I can tell and I understood more than I saw; for I was seeing in a sacred manner the shapes of all things in the spirit, and the shape of all shapes as they must live together like one being. And I saw that the sacred hoop of my people was one of many hoops that made one circle…And I saw that it was holy." Black Elk then dedicated his life to helping his people as a medicine man, sharing his visions and performing healing ceremonies for the sick and dispirited during the fateful years that witnessed repeated clashes between the Plains tribes and government troops. But eventually he realized that all the power he was given was useless, at least for the time, for after the massacre by government soldiers at Wounded Knee in 1890, his people were forced onto the Pine Ridge reservation. "A people's dream died there," he recalled. "It was a beautiful dream." Sadly Black Elk concluded that "There is no center any longer, and the sacred tree is dead."

But Black Elk continued to share his knowledge, visions, and spiritual practices even with the dominant culture that oppressed his own people. Well into the twentieth century, he taught others the mystery and holiness of the sacred circle.

THE ART OF THE MUSHROOM

The Mazatec shaman Maria Sabina was born in 1894 to a poor family in Mexico. Her life was one of suffering and poverty, yet hundreds of people sought her help in overcoming their own illnesses and sorrows. Maria Sabina practiced the ancient art of the mushroom. As she said, "The sacred mushroom takes me by the hand and brings me to the world where everything is known." This is a "world that talks…[that] has a language of its own. I report what it says."

For Sabina the mushroom was a sacrament, a friend, something "similar to your soul…[and] takes you where the soul wants to go." But not everyone, she pointed out, who takes the mushroom has visions that serve a useful purpose. They do not work for everyone. Only shamans who have an intimate friendship with the mushroom can serve others by the visions that the mushroom, or any psychoactive plant, gives them.

The world of nonordinary reality that Sabina entered during her ecstatic states is a place where she can "see our past and our future, which are there together as a single thing already achieved, already happened." As a shaman, she made many journeys into that realm. "The more you go inside the world of *teo-nanacatl* [the mushroom], the more things are seen."

Sabina's shamanic practice was a blend of indigenous and Christian traditions. Meso-America has been Catholic for more than three hundred years, and the ancient spirituality of the mushroom and the newer Christian religion infused her journeys. Traditionally the mushroom was known as the Flesh of God, and in Christian times it has been considered the Blood of Christ. For Maria Sabina, knowledge from the mushroom was the Word of God. The two traditions were not at loggerheads with each other but formed a seamless whole for her work. Shamans, like Sabina, who have visions of the essential unity of the spirit world, often find no conflict in incorporating both native and Christian spirituality into their work.

For example, while Sabina was in a trance from the mushroom, she chanted lines such as the following:

> Woman who waits am I, Woman who divines am I...
> I am a daughter of Christ, a daughter of Mary...
> Lawyer woman am I, eagle woman am I,
> opossum woman am I...Clock woman am I,
> Whirling woman of the whirlwind am I...
> Woman of a sacred, enchanted place am I.

She also called on the Christian saints, as in the following:

> Saint Peter, Saint Paul, shout, you! whistle, you!
> I am going to thunder,
> I am going to sound.

The knowledge that Sabina received in her journeys into the world of the mushroom gave her practical healing advice for others. Once, when working to heal her uncle, she asked the mushroom spirits what herbs he needed since the herbal remedies that the local *curanderos* (healers) had prescribed had not worked. She asked the spirits, and "they told me that an evil spirit had entered the blood of my uncle and to cure him we should give him some [special] herbs." She asked where these herbs grew, and the spirits "took me to a place on the mountain where tall trees grew and the waters of the brook ran, and they showed me the herbs that I should pull from the earth and the road that I had to take to find them." When she returned from her spirit journey in nonordinary reality, she left her village and went to the place in ordinary reality that the spirits had shown her, found the herb, brought it back, and administered it to her uncle, who was cured in a few days.

PLANT SPIRIT MEDICINE

Shamanic practitioner Eliot Cowan is calling shamanic healers to return to the ancient practice of working directly with the spirits to learn which plants can be used in healing. But it is more than just knowing which herbal remedies relieve which conditions. He relates the story of a Westerner walking a jungle trail through the Amazon with a shaman, learning from him the different medicinal plants that grew there and what healing powers they contained. Later, back in the village, the Westerner asked the shaman to repeat the information about collecting, preparing, and using the different plants so that he could write it down in his notebook. The shaman laughed and replied that he was only introducing the Westerner to some plants, not pre-scribing them. To know which plants to use and how to administer them, he said, "the spirit of the plant must come to you in your dreams…[and tell you] how to prepare it and what it will cure." Only then can it be used effectively.

A student of acupuncture and Chinese medicine, Cowan is also an apprentice and the designated successor of Don Guadalupe González Ríos, a Huichol shaman. In his healing practice, Cowan advocates working with the spirits of the plants, an approach he calls "one of the great medical traditions of the planet." While not denying that certain plants have healing properties for specific ailments, Cowan focuses attention on the shaman's concern, namely, that the healer and patient honor and work with the living intelligence of the plant itself. He reminds us that "every plant is a miracle and a mystery."

Cowan's own healing practice and the tradition that he imparts to his students is firmly rooted in the shamanic wisdom of the centuries. He recommends dreams, pilgrimages, and vision quests as the shaman's source of knowledge, along with the journey to the lower world to actively meet and learn from the plant spirits. He tells us that the spirits of plants are willing to teach and heal human beings, as are the five elements, which, from Cowan's Chinese perspective, are earth, fire, water, wood, and metal.

Most importantly, according to Cowan, the healer must ask the plants directly if they can be used for certain illnesses and certain patients. Healers must also be willing to personalize and individualize treatments, breaking out of their familiar routine, and not simply "go by the book." Only then can they tap into the mystery and miraculous power of plant medicine. Finally, both the healer and the patient must work in a spirit of humility and gratitude, acknowledging dependence upon and partnership with the nonhuman elements of the Earth. As Cowan puts it, "The dream of nature is a complex web of mutuality in which each part supports the other." In brief, healing takes place in a relationship based on friendship with the spirit world and the helping spirits of nature, because as Cowan puts it, "there is only one active ingredient in plant medicines—friendship."

HEALING THROUGH ANCESTRAL MEMORIES

As shamans explore the mysteries of plants and personal visions of the universe, they do not operate alone, but within a web of ancestral power and wisdom. Being in touch with the ancestors is of primary importance for successful shamanizing. The story of Malidoma Somé's training and initiation into shamanic mysteries highlights this.

Somé, a Dagara shaman from West Africa, was kidnapped out of his village by French Jesuits when he was four years old and educated in a mission school and Jesuit seminary for the next fifteen years. When he realized he could endure no more, he fled through the jungle and walked for five days to cover the many miles back to his family's village. Because he had missed the initiation rites that usually occur at puberty, Somé was told by elders that he would have to undergo the rigorous rites of passage even though he was an adult. It would be exceptionally difficult for him because, as they put it, he had lost the part of his spirit connected to the ancestral world. In its place was the restless spirit animating Western civilization, a spirit that is "tense and uneasy...scared...made of terror," the restlessness of what Somé's people call the "spirit of the white man." Somé's father told him that "the elders want to quiet the white man in your soul."

For Somé, reclaiming the ancestral soul is a process of drumming, journeying, and spending time with the spirits of nature. Somé points out that "the drum is a transportation device that carries the listener into other worlds" and "to forget how to drum is to forget how to feel." By reconnecting with those feelings and journeying into the spirit realms, Somé was initiated into shamanhood by learning how to "act upon one's own memory...to recall what I already knew." He learned that the spirit and the mind are one, and that together they perceive a reality that is "much greater than the vision we experience in the ordinary world." Initiation for the shaman is to learn how to trust that knowing, to welcome and evaluate the information received from the ancestors, who now inhabit other worlds of reality. As Somé puts it, the mind "does not make things up. It can't imagine what does not exist."

Shamans who have not broken with their traditional lifeways are to a great extent still connected to the ancestral world. Most Western shamanic practitioners, however, like Malidoma Somé returning from fifteen years of Western education, have been so conditioned by the restless, materialistic, tense world of modern life that it can be difficult to break that control over the mind and soul and return to the ways of the ancestors. Indeed, many practitioners don't know who their ancestors are and may require years of journeying and instruction from the spirits to rediscover that part of their soul that "remembers." The words of the elder who trained Somé apply to all shamans and shamanic practitioners: "Live as [a person] who remembers. You cannot be who you truly are until you can put what you remember into action in your life...You must remember. Remembering means submitting to your fate." And the way to remember is to journey with the ancestors, the spirits of those who have gone before us and yet still remain in the fields, forests, mountains, rivers, and the many sacred places of the land.

STORY, SONG, AND DANCE

Northwest Coast shaman, medicine man, and storyteller Johnny Moses challenges people to find some tradition that will reconnect them with the Earth. He says, "If you don't have a tradition, adopt one. If you don't have any elders, adopt an elder." Moses is a goodwill ambassador for several Northwest Coast native traditions in which he was raised. His mission is to encourage people of all backgrounds to "communicate with the Earth, to love the Earth, and to give back to the Earth."

Moses was born in a Nootka village on Vancouver Island, British Columbia, and raised by his maternal grandparents until he was nine, when he was sent to a Catholic boarding school. Diagnosed with cancer at age twelve, and not responding to chemotherapy, radiology, and surgery that took one lung and parts of his stomach, he was sent home to die. But family healers and medicine people brought Moses back to health. "It took about a month," he says. Subsequent X-rays showed no sign of cancer. It was at this time that his grandmother gave him the name Whis.stem.men.knee, which means "Walking Medicine Robe."

Moses travels around the world and inspires healing communities, which are collectively called the Red Cedar Circle. In these gatherings, people come together for the healing and rejuvenating effects of storytelling, song, and dance. For Moses, being a shaman is being a storyteller, and native stories are considered "teachings." Stories are also healers.

Moses sees all created things as sacred, alive, and related to one another. In his stories animals, birds, mountains, and trees think of themselves as "people" with "life and feelings" that have much to teach human beings, whom, as Moses wryly points out, also "think they are people."

In addition to stories, singing and dancing "are ways of worshipping and of healing ourselves," says Moses. Dance is "both a spiritual and physical prayer." Some dancers stomp their feet to the drum's beat, "connecting our spiritual roots with Mother Earth's roots, her veins." In other dances, people spin to "untie and regenerate" themselves. Moses explains, "We get dizzy from spinning, but afterwards we see things differently."

Song is also an important part of Moses's healing ceremonies. "A tree might give you a song, or a rock or the water" in the same ways that "lullabies are songs given to us by the babies." From Moses's shamanic point of view, it is important for people to have a relationship with the spirits of nature—to listen and hear them—for they give us the songs, stories, dances, and healing messages that can restore our lives. "We know the spirits and ancestors are always there in the forests and mountains, waiting for us to visit them, but we are the ones who have to visit," Moses explains.

Visiting the spirits of nature for a vision is a "sacred art" for Moses. A potential vision quester prepares by enduring hardships, such as bathing in ice-cold water, fasting, staying awake, and practicing acts of patience. "In medicine work, we have to suffer to make ourselves strong," Moses explains. "A spirit power usually comes to you through your dreams or in your thoughts when you are fasting or praying."

All spirit power, according to Moses, is "the healing spirit of God, which is the love of God." If people establish this relationship first, he says, then later they can work with the spirits of animals and plants. In Moses's vision all creatures carry the same spirit. If people are patient, the spirit will come to them, perhaps in the form of an animal, a plant, a mountain, or even in a talent such as hunting, cooking, or storytelling. When people trust in the healing power and love of the Creator, Moses says, "then they can see clearly that the love they carry is the same love the trees and the animals have inside them; their soul is the same...I was healed with love—what we call the Great Mystery."

SOUL RETRIEVAL

One of the primary services performed by shamans is soul retrieval—the search to recover and restore a person's vital essence when it has been lost or stolen. From a shamanic point of view, physical and emotional illness, as well as misfortune, are due to loss of personal power or life force, the diminution of the spirit that keep us alive and strong. In indigenous cultures it is often believed that the soul may wander at night during sleep and be stolen by a vengeful sorcerer or captured by a wounded animal in need of strength and health. In many places people fear that the soul of someone recently deceased may latch onto the soul of the living and sap its vital essence in attempts to remain alive in this reality. Shamans and shamanic practitioners can rescue such souls, retrieve, and restore them.

The Huichol shaman Ramón Medina Silva explains that when he does a soul retrieval, he searches for "that life—the soul, consciousness, life energy. In his vision, he hunts "to see where 'that life' was lost. To see where it is lying, frightened. Where it is in danger" He says the shaman "goes listening, listening. To see where 'that life' was dropped." The soul might be "under a branch, or under a leaf, or under a small stone." When he finds it, he whistles to it softly, gently picks it up with his feathered plumes, places it in a wad of cotton, and brings it back so he can restore the sick person to health. Silva's technique is one of many found worldwide.

In recent years, Sandra Ingerman has emerged as the foremost authority on modern soul retrieval techniques based on core shamanic practices found in classical shamanism. As a shamanic practitioner with a professional background in psychotherapy, Ingerman began recognizing in her clients' descriptions of trauma, abuse, physical accidents, mourning, and depression elements of what in shamanic cultures would be seen as soul loss. Clients often told her that they didn't feel "whole" or "complete," as if "part of me is missing" or "not all there." Often this feeling was connected to a death, divorce, rape, surgery, childhood abuse, physical trauma, addiction, severe illness, or ongoing depression. In the face of these traumatic events, the part of the soul that suffers may leave. As Ingerman puts it, "Soul loss is the way the psyche of a person can survive a painful event…Unfortunately, psychology doesn't ask where parts of a person's consciousness go when they dissociate." The shaman does.

As Ingerman listened to clients present their symptoms, she decided to use shamanic journeys into nonordinary reality to ask her own power animals and helping spirits how to best serve her clients. A firm believer in the power of healing that comes from another person being willing to intervene in the spiritual realms for someone else, Ingerman began to journey for the purpose of finding, bringing back, and restoring "that life" to her clients. Ingerman began to specialize in soul retrieval in her shamanic practice and teaching.

Bringing back a lost soul or part of a soul is not a quick fix. Ingerman stresses with her clients and the shamanic practitioners she trains that integrating the returned soul, making it feel "at home," is critical for recovery. Often clients must learn to journey themselves and begin deep and productive relationships with the restored soul parts. In other words, the client must also become a practitioner of shamanic healing. Convinced that "it's vitally important for shamanism to be adapted to the society in which it's practiced," Ingerman believes that soul retrieval is only the first step in putting the person back on the soul's journey through life. Shamanic perspectives on health and wholeness must become part of the client's daily outlook if the person hopes to mend what Ingerman calls "the fragmented self."

EXTRACTIONS

Since the shamanic theory of health and illness focuses on personal power, illness results when a person's spiritual power is diminished in some way or when an individual loses spiritual power or soul. The illness moves into the "gap" in the person's life force, bringing patterns of energy that are harmful for the individual. Extraction is the shamanic healing method in which the shaman locates a harmful spiritual intrusion in the sick person's body and removes it. An intrusion is something like an infection in Western medical terms. Extractions can be done with the hand or mouth; sometimes a power object, such as a feather, stone, stick, or rattle, is also used to lure or attract the intrusion and bring it up and out of the body.

Essie Parrish, a Pomo shaman in northern California, was one of the most famous extraction healers of the twentieth century. She used mouth-sucking techniques that are found in many parts of the world. Parrish could both see and hear the intrusion. She would call on "Our Father" as her source of power, incorporating Christian ideas she acquired as a member of the Church of Latter-Day Saints. The power "comes down into me," she said, and then she sees the harmful intrusion "way inside the sick person lying there…That disease that comes down into a person is dirty."

Parrish could "hear the disease making noise…just like insects." She would stretch her hand over the person's body and feel the disease pulling her palm and middle finger "like a magnet." "The pain sitting somewhere inside the person feels like it is pulling your hand toward itself," she explained. Then Parrish would suck the disease out of the patient into her mouth. "I spit out the dead disease…and put it in something like a piece of paper or a basket," where it disappears.

For most shamanic healers, the extraction process usually involves going into a shamanic state of consciousness, summoning one's helping spirits, and building up personal power in order to confront the intruding power successfully. Then the shaman finds the location of the intrusion in the body by seeing, hearing, or feeling it with the hand. The actual extraction can involve sucking directly on the skin, through the clothing, or through the hands cupped over the appropriate area on the person's body. It can also be removed by pulling, rubbing, or grasping the intrusion with the hands either physically touching the body or working in the energy field a few inches above the body. Some shamans tap and flick the intrusion out with a feather, rattle, stick, or stone. When the intrusion is removed, it is put into some neutral place, such as a bowl of water or sand or into a river or other natural body of water, where it dissipates back into the universe.

An extraction method used in the Scottish Highlands begins with the healer placing both palms on the ground or floor to make contact with Earth, the source of healing and energy. Then the healer "grasps and clutches and fingers and rubs the patient to and fro, up and down, this way and that, hither and thither." The physical treatment, however, is only part of the cure, for, as a Scottish healer explains, "to do this work right is the work of hands and head and heart."

With head and heart, the healer invokes the spirits by reciting the following chant (or one of many variations) addressed to the illness. The words intimidate the spirit of the illness by boasting of the many personal relationships the healer has with the elemental spirits in nature that will come to drive out the illness and help heal the sick individual.

> Power of moon have I over you,
> Power of sun have I over you,
> Power of rain have I over you,
> Power of dew have I over you,
> Power of sea have I over you,

Power of land have I over you,
Power of stars have I over you,
Power of planets have I over you,
Power of universe have I over you,
Power of skies have I over you,
Power of saints have I over you,
Power of heaven and the worlds have I over you,
Power of heaven and power of God have I over you.

Then the healer sends the illness out into the universe, where it will be carried away. There are two methods for this. One is to put "part of" the illness into places or animals remote from human habitation and capable of "carrying" a portion of the illness without harming themselves:

A part of you on the gray stones,
A part of you on the steep mountains,
A part of you on the swift cascades,
A part of you on the gleaming clouds,
A part of you on the ocean-whales,
A part of you on the meadow-beasts,
A part of you on the fenny swamps,
A part of you on the cotton-grass moors,
A part of you on the great surging sea—
She herself has the best means to carry [you far away].
She herself has the best means to carry.

The second method is to send the illness to nine hills, naming each hill specifically, such as "Be this illness on the Hill of Diarmaid" or "Be this illness on the Hill of the Hunts." The idea is to remove the spirit of the illness and send it away from the human being, where it does not belong.

SOUL ESCORTING

Near-death experiences related by countless men and women attest to the presence of a radiant, beautiful light that beckons them and through which they must pass to cross over into the next world. As Malidoma Somé puts it, "The light we encounter on the road of death is...our natural state, but...we human beings must help each other as we move toward the shores of light." Shamans and shamanic practitioners have been doing that for centuries. They are psychopomps, or soul escorts.

There are various reasons why a recently deceased person may not move toward the light. In some cultures it is thought that demons and other contrary spirits block the soul's path. In some places a person who dies from a disease is considered to be at risk of not ascending into the light but of being pulled down and caught in the Earthly realms. Seance mediums consistently report that a person whose life is unexpectedly or violently interrupted, such as in a car accident, fire, or war, may find it difficult to leave the place where his or her body remains. Mediums also encounter spirits who are still inordinately attached to something in this life, such as a home or a business project. Some people want to stay around to help loved ones or get revenge against their enemies. Fear of leaving family and friends behind can also keep a spirit attached to this life. Any of these situations can encourage a spirit to haunt the area where it lived and not move into the next life quickly and comfortably.

Shamans can help souls cross over to the other side because they know the terrain of the spirit world and may even have journeyed through the realms where the dead pass. They also know how to find lost souls and bring them back or escort them into other places. Many cultures have elaborate funeral ceremonies in which the shaman plays a key role in releasing the spirit of the deceased. In Siberia, for example, a funerary ritual can last seven days, involving the relatives of the deceased, considerable feasting, drinking, music, dancing, and drumming, with the shaman singing his journeys into the spirit world and relating his efforts to help the deceased reach the heavenly realms. Part of the shaman's task is to lead the soul to its relatives who have passed on and are waiting for the newcomer.

An Irish woman trained in shamanism by her grandmother in the 1950s has described her methods of escorting souls into the next world, noting that alleviating the spirit's fear is the first step in helping it to move on. "Fear hangs around the doorways [to the other world]," said the woman, who asked to remain anonymous. "Entities like me, we gang up on the other side of the door." Then she and the other spirits "pour so much light" into the spirit that "the old fear doesn't have a prayer." As the deceased rises into the air, the shamans keep surrounding the soul in light. After people die, she said, "they are looking for their loved ones, or they are looking for something they have imagined in their minds. You have to overcome any punitive or negative idea that they may have had about the Afterworld." She explained that she will look around for the parents of the deceased if they have already died and "rush them over there like the ambulance with the sirens going…to welcome them [the deceased] into the Otherworld." Her experiences as a psychopomp, unlike those described by some tribal shamans as dangerous and frightening, are "exciting…you feel so good when you do this…because you're taking that

soul out of this small, limited existence into such an e
ed light-being consciousness." As Malidoma Somé
"The light is where we belong."

From this brief overview of shamanic work, it is clear that
the mystery of life will never cease to present challenges to
human beings to utilize shamanic techniques for healing
and understanding the nature of the universe. All the
women and men presented here take responsibility for their
lives and the lives and well-being of those who come to
them for help. Shamanism is about taking responsibility for
all the realities in which we live. Don Juan, Carlos
Casteñada's Huichol teacher, puts it this way:

> For me the world is stupendous, awesome, myste-
> rious, unfathomable...You must assume responsi-
> bility for being here, in this marvelous world, in
> this marvelous desert, in this marvelous time.

Chapter Four:
How to Find and Work with a Shaman or Shamanic Practitioner

People visit shamans and shamanic practitioners primarily for healing, divination, and advice on important life issues. This chapter offers guidelines for finding and working with both shamans and shamanic practitioners, understanding and evaluating their approaches, and integrating their services into your life.

FINDING AND WORKING WITH A TRADITIONAL SHAMAN

It isn't easy to visit a traditional shaman. In fact, it has been said, somewhat facetiously but with a ring of truth, that shamans intentionally make it difficult for non-indigenous people to see them for healing work. With the growing interest in native healing practices and spiritual work in the last thirty years, it makes sense that traditional shamans would become circumspect about outsiders approaching them. Many people from dominant cultures come out of idle curiosity or for self-aggrandizement, hoping to have a "session" with a shaman in order to impress others back home or to present themselves as having acquired special knowledge or powers from a shaman. Furthermore, indigenous shamans are busy, spending most of their time in healing work within their own communities and often holding down regular jobs as well.

Using a Go-between

Most likely you will need a go-between or mediator to arrange a consultation visit or a healing session with a shaman. This may be someone from the shaman's community or an outsider whom the shaman trusts and respects and who has done mediating work between the shaman and outsiders before. It is in your interests to have a go-between for a number of reasons.

Many indigenous shamans live in remote areas where their communities have resided for centuries or on distant reservation lands where they have been forced to live by the encroachment of modern civilization. A mediator will know where the shaman lives and how to get there, which might involve a difficult trek on hard-to-follow roads and into areas not always found on commercial maps. But even if the shaman lives in town and is listed in a phone book, it is still wise to respect his or her privacy and have someone known to the shaman make the initial overture.

Indigenous cultures have strict standards of protocol and etiquette of which outsiders are usually ignorant. A mediator can explain the correct and polite way to approach a native healer. For example, there may be traditional forms of address, such as "Grandmother" or "Uncle," that should be used. On the other hand, native people may use these terms of address but would think it improper for non-natives to do so. Also, it may or may not be proper to use the shaman's first name. There may be certain seasons, days, and times of day that the shaman devotes to seeing people, and these should be observed carefully. It would be impolite to show up unexpectedly. In fact, usually the mediator will tell the shaman who you are and what kind of help you are seeking before he or she will agree to meet with you.

Gifts and Payments

Native cultures place great stock in gift-giving. It is customary to bring a gift when first meeting a shaman, and other gifts on successive sessions. Tobacco is a common gift among many Native Americans. Many people also give food, if not for the shaman specifically, then for his or her people on the reservation or in the community. Since indigenous communities have a high rate of unemployment and poverty, food that a shaman can distribute to needy neighbors is always a welcome gift. It is best to ask the mediator about the proper gift-giving traditions for the shaman you plan to see.

Money payments for healing services vary from shaman to shaman. Traditionally, native healers did not take money for services, but within their traditions, patients compensated for healing and other services with items of great value, such as blankets, food, tools, clothing, even horses.

Most shamans, especially in North America, no longer live in a barter society. They live in a capitalist economy just like everyone else and need money to pay bills and buy groceries. Nevertheless, some traditional shamans refuse to accept money for their services, while others do. A mediator who is familiar with the practices of the shaman you hope to see can tell you what it will cost, or what is expected of you in lieu of money.

Preparing Yourself to Visit a Traditional Shaman

It is hard for people brought up in a mainstream culture to know what to expect and how to integrate the services offered by a traditional shaman. It is probably best to say that you should be ready for anything, but obviously not ready to accept or do just anything! Shamans vary in skills, competencies, and expertise, just like any other healers or health-care providers in the Western medical profession and in alternative systems. Some are better than others. You should definitely try to find references if possible, people from your own background who have gone to the shaman and can report on his or her effectiveness and honesty. If you know the mediator well, you can ask him or her to tell you what to expect. You might also seek out any books or articles about the shaman or read about his or her culture.

Before your visit, it is essential to become clear within yourself about your motives and reasons for wanting to consult with the shaman. In fact, the shaman may test you first to determine whether you are honest and sincere about being healed, or just a curiosity seeker. The great Native American healer Rolling Thunder would question would-be patients about their motives. "Why do you want to be relieved of this condition?" he would ask. "Do you just want to feel better, or what are you going to do? Is there anything else that you would like to improve or change? Is there anything else you would like to say? Because whatever you say now, that's the way it's going to be." These are the kind of questions you should consider before you go to see a shaman for healing. Shamans believe that the reasons you want to be healed are crucial to being healed. Sometimes implied in their questions is their desire to know whether you are planning to change your life for the better and not return to the destructive lifestyle that brought on the condition in the first place.

Shamans work from a holistic point of view, seeking to restore balance and harmony both in the lives of their patients and in the cosmos itself, since the two are intimately linked. The shaman views all life in terms of personal relationships: friendship, gift-giving, respect, mutual support, and love. Although this may sound mystical, shamans also tend to blend practical methods and advice with spiritual activities. You may, for example, be told to change your diet and get more exercise, in addition to carrying a particular charm, making a fetish, or saying a prayer to the stars or the wind. Shamanic healing is holistic in that it looks at body, mind, spirit, soul, environment, and living arrangements. The shaman often can see many dimensions in your life that are related to your problem and will offer suggestions that address those areas, even though you may not always see the connections.

Evaluating a Shaman's Advice

It is important to enter into the shaman's world view as much as possible for healing to occur. At the same time, you need to evaluate the shaman's recommendations and not accept them uncritically, just as you would a diagnosis given by a Western medical provider. It is not out of line to ask questions, seek information from others, or even get "second opinions." In other words, check out the advice that you are given with others who are familiar with native healing practices. At the same time, keep in mind that each shaman has unique and personal approaches to healing based on the information given by the shaman's personal helping spirits. There are not always "standard" practices with which to compare shamans. Being treated by a traditional shaman requires a certain amount of common sense on your part, while allowing for the fact that native ways are unfamiliar to you. If a shaman recommends some treatment, ritual, or medicine that seems wrong or dangerous, seek additional advice from others.

The same warning applies to the length of time a shaman works with you. There is no way to predict how long or often you will have to see the shaman. Of course, this is true with psychotherapy and other Western healing modalities as well. To complicate the issue, shamanic healing often works primarily on the spiritual level, rather than directly with the physical problems that initially brought you to the shaman. Again, the principle involved here is holistic. The shaman sees all aspects of a person's life as interconnected and influencing one another. The results from shamanic healing may be subtle and not readily apparent on the physical level. On some occasions, however, the effects of a shaman's work are immediate and dramatic, even miraculous. But more often, the healing occurs gradually and in conjunction with other remedies you may be employing. This can make it difficult to evaluate whether you are improving from the shaman's work or not, and to decide whether to continue with your visits.

Opening Your Mind and Heart for Shamanic Healing

Much has been written about the placebo effect both in Western medicine and in alternative modalities. Essentially, the placebo effect indicates that patients recover to some extent in relation to their belief in the treatment, whether the remedy be taking prescription medicine from a medical doctor, receiving spinal adjustments from a chiropractor, or carrying a crystal provided by a native healer. This can make it tricky to evaluate a shaman's work. You have to accept the treatment and remedies and "believe" in them, even though they may seem alien to you and be based on a belief system that contradicts assumptions that have been part of your world view since childhood. At the same time, you may harbor a certain amount of disbelief accompanied by a prove-it-to-me attitude. How can you achieve the right attitude so that you can benefit from shamanic healing?

Probably the best advice is to maintain an open mind and heart to what the shaman tells you, while at the same time trying not to reject all your previous notions about illness and recovery. Many people discover that while they may have doubts about a specific treatment recommended by a shaman, they have faith in the shaman's overall approach because they realize that Western medicine frequently ignores the spiritual causes of illness and misfortune, and that this is precisely where the shaman can provide the needed balance. This generalized belief in shamanic work, if strong enough, may override your specific doubts about the efficacy of individual practices.

When all is said and done, illness and healing are mysterious processes that play important roles in our lives. We cannot always understand what causes them, what they mean, or why they happen to us. Often it can be difficult to know when to resist and when to go with the flow of things, when to fight and when to surrender to the inevitable.

These are individual judgment calls and are not easy to make. Shamans are often very pragmatic people, not claiming that their methods are the only ones that work. They frequently employ Western medicine as well as their own traditional procedures. You probably should too, accepting that each approach offers something the other may overlook, and acknowledging that your problem may require several concurrent practices for healing to take place on all levels.

FINDING AND WORKING WITH A SHAMANIC PRACTITIONER

There are many similarities in working with shamans and shamanic practitioners, but there are also some significant differences. Following are some guidelines for engaging the services of a shamanic practitioner.

How to Find a Shamanic Practitioner

Unlike traditional shamans, who may want to preserve their privacy and not become celebrities, shamanic practitioners usually want to be recognized and often put great effort into promoting themselves and their work. In comparison with native shamans, some modern practitioners may seem crass or materialistic in their self-promotion, but there are several reasons why such advertising is necessary.

The mainstream culture does not promote alternative healing work, and shamanic practitioners often feel invisible. Most people have never heard of shamanism, or if they have, they still think that shamanic healers can be found only in indigenous or exotic communities. Practitioners therefore have a double hurdle: to make themselves known to people in their communities and, at the same time, to educate them about shamanism. Traditional shamans have neither of these problems, for they are well known among their people, and communities that have not abandoned their ancestral ways know what shamanic work is all about.

Shamanic practitioners sometimes advertise in New Age journals and publications. Some leave flyers or business cards at local healing centers, health food stores, or community centers that support alternative healing and spiritual work. It is not always easy to evaluate shamanic practitioners by their ads. Many sound the same; some are too brief to give a clear sense of what the shamanic practitioner actually does; others are quite lengthy but are written in vague "spirit-babble" that doesn't say anything specific. Because of these problems it is best to call the practitioner, explain the reasons you are seeking an appointment, and ask about his or her approach and techniques in working with the issues that concern you. A phone conversation can give you (and the practitioner) a chance to begin to evaluate whether the two of you will be able to work well together. A practitioner who doesn't think she or he can help you should be able to refer you to someone who can.

Evaluating a Practitioner's Methods

There are no accrediting agencies for shamanic practitioners similar to those for mainstream professions, and there probably never will be due to the individualized nature of shamanism and the fact that some practitioners, just as in tribal cultures, have a natural facility as healers with or without extensive formal training. Some recognized teachers of shamanism have established training courses and present certificates to students who complete the training, but this is not the same as accrediting them as shamans. It simply gives the public information about the tradition, approach, and extent of study that the practitioner has completed and shows that, in the eyes of the teacher or the foundation, the practitioner has successfully completed the training program and has permission to include that information in a résumé.

Shamanic practitioners tend to be eclectic. Even those who have studied extensively in one tradition or have been apprenticed to a specific shaman often incorporate other practices in their work. Again, the pragmatic nature of shamanism in general prepares a practitioner to be open-minded to other approaches. This is also true of traditional shamans, who do not claim that their techniques are the only ways to be healed or to gather information.

Eclecticism appeals to shamanic practitioners for other reasons as well. Many want to provide a large repertoire of healing techniques to clients on the assumption that some good can come from all of them and different clients may need different combinations of help. Eclecticism also makes good business sense. To survive in a culture that does not recognize shamanism (and can be hostile toward it), the more healing services you can offer your clients the better. Shamanic practitioners, for example, may incorporate massage therapy, herbalism, foot reflexology, and Jungian dreamwork in their practice. A professional psychotherapist may use shamanism in therapy sessions along with standard psychotherapeutic techniques.

On the other hand, being certified in several or many healing methods does not make a person a better shamanic practitioner. You must still evaluate practitioners on their shamanic knowledge and skills. So, if possible, find out who a practitioner's primary teachers are and how long he or she has studied with them. Also ask how long the practitioner has been practicing shamanism. As mentioned above, the length of study or practice is not always an accurate indicator of how good a practitioner is since some people have a natural affinity for shamanic work and learn quickly. Similarly, many years of practice do not necessarily make a practitioner better than someone who is newer in the field. But in general, knowing who the practitioners' teachers were, what tradition or approach they take in their practice, and how long they have been working as shamanic practitioners can help in evaluating them.

As with traditional shamans, ask for references: people who know the practitioners personally or who have gone to them professionally. While teachers, courses of training, and number of years practicing can give you some insight into practitioners' abilities, they cannot attest to their honesty and integrity. Only firsthand accounts from people who know them can provide this information.

Finally, in deciding to proceed with a practitioner, it is good to get a sense of how that practitioner views your situation in terms of his or her ability to help and the length of time it may take. While the outcome of a healing process is hardly ever predictable, you have a right to ask the practitioner about these issues. You have a right to know, for example, if the practitioner plans on a series of sessions that will last for several weeks or months. There are not many "quick fixes" when it comes to healing, even though once in a while there are miraculous recoveries. You should expect that more than one visit will be necessary. Even though the practitioner cannot foretell how quickly the sessions will bring improvement in your situation, you should ask for some good-faith estimate about the length of the healing program you are about to embark on.

Gifts and Payments

Shamanic practitioners may charge money for sessions or may ask for some kind of nonmonetary exchange. Usually practitioners who are raised in capitalist cultures find no problem with accepting money for their services. Even though they may see themselves as channels of healing power from the spirits, they know that if they are not paid, they will have to use that time in some other kind of employment and not be able to do shamanic work. Some practitioners charge regular fees per hour or session; some use a sliding scale and let the client decide how much he or she can afford.

Some practitioners barter or ask for "exchanges" in lieu of monetary payments. Exchanges are often done with other alternative healers or spiritual workers—for example, exchanging a divination journey for a massage or soul retrieval work for a series of polarity sessions. Sometimes clients who do not have extra money for shamanic work may barter other kinds of services, such as chopping firewood, cutting grass, or doing some typing. A practitioner and client should work out the details to make the exchange fair and reasonable.

It is important that some kind of payment be made, especially for ongoing work involving multiple sessions. Without it, the client falls into "psychic debt," which can be harmful to both parties. The client knows, perhaps only subliminally, that he or she is in debt and owes the practitioner something in return. As sessions go by, the practitioner realizes that the client takes up time, energy, and psychic commitment without giving anything in return. Eventually a practitioner may grow to resent the time and energy that could be spent on clients or other work projects that would make money.

Keeping an Open Mind and Heart

As when working with a traditional shaman, a client seeking a shamanic practitioner should keep an open mind and heart, but tempered by good judgment. Shamanic practitioners are not authorities on all alternative healing remedies, though some clients with very little knowledge of holistic healing mistakenly assume that people who work in the field are experts on all aspects of healing. Even the more eclectic practitioners who offer a range of healing modalities may not be well versed in all of them.

As with a traditional shaman, you may have to "stretch" your beliefs somewhat to accommodate the world view and principles on which shamanic healing is based. There are examples, of course, of skeptics and debunkers being healed in spite of themselves, but a prove-it-to-me attitude is usually not the frame of mind conducive to healing. Go to a shamanic practitioner with trust and openness, but do not disregard common sense. Try to see the practitioner's view of illness, healing, spiritual help, and the nature of the universe as necessary for him or her to do the work. To the extent that you can enter into this framework of beliefs and values you will facilitate your own healing.

When consulting a shamanic practitioner for divination work, such as dream interpretation or advice on decisionmaking, go with an open heart and mind but retain good judgment. Similar to psychic readers, shamanic practitioners use their abilities to access information not readily available under ordinary circumstances, usually by asking their helping spirits and relaying the information to the client. As with other forms of divination, the psychic or adviser may or may not have clear insight into the client's situation. An honest practitioner will say, "I'm not sure what this information means" or "I really don't know the best way to interpret this for you." Sometimes it is not necessary to interpret the information because the practitioner is merely conveying it from the spirits, and it is up to the client to reflect or meditate on it for the meaning; on other occasions the practitioner may get strong feelings or insights about what the information means or what the client "should" do and may tell the client.

Treat all information as you would advice from a close friend or family member and evaluate it critically and carefully. Just because information comes from the spirit world does not mean that it is necessarily accurate or appropriate. It may be based on faulty assumptions, or the spirits may not have all the information needed to make a decision, or you or the practitioner may misinterpret the information. While trusting that the practitioner has done his or her best, use your own intuition and judgment before actually making changes in your life based on the information the shamanic practitioner gave you.

It has been said in many cultures, in many ways, that our nature and the nature of the universe are the same. If we are ailing, so is the Earth. If we recover, our healing comes from the Earth. Shamanism is a method for strengthening the spirit between us and the rest of Creation. For whatever reasons a person seeks help from those who practice shamanism, results occur only when the seeker becomes reconnected to the flow of divine energy that is the life force of Creation.

Chapter Five:
How to Pursue Shamanic Training and Practice

Your interest in shamanism may go beyond the merely intellectual. You may be reading this book for deeper, more personal reasons, perhaps wondering if you are being called to practice shamanism yourself. How do you know if shamanism is a credible path for you to follow?

HEARING THE CALL

Even candidates in tribal cultures may be confused by the call or the influence of spirits in their lives, and they seek out elders to help them understand what is being asked of them. Following are some general guidelines to help you determine if you have a shamanic calling. But just as in indigenous cultures, it is helpful to discuss your personal experiences and expectations with someone knowledgeable in shamanism and shamanic practice.

Early Indications

Many current practitioners of shamanism indicate that they knew from childhood or early adolescence that they were being called to something different in terms of healing work or spiritual practice. Their early interest in nature, psychic phenomena, or magical and mystical experiences was, in hindsight, a kind of introduction to what they would later discover is shamanism. Often these early predilections alert individuals that there is something "more" to reality than they are learning from parents and teachers.

A deeper, more mystical interest in nature is often an indication that the spirits are calling you to shamanic work. At first the interest might be quite ordinary, such as an affinity for camping, canoeing, hiking, bird watching, star gazing, or sailing, but later you may discover that your relationship to nature and the elements is different than other people's. In fact, it may be perceived as something that cannot be shared with others because they would not understand or they would think you were slightly crazy. Your perceptions might include recognizing a spirit, intelligence, or consciousness present in nature, a perception that friends and family members do not share.

Many people relate a "tingle" experience with the word *shaman* or with experiences that involve shamanic terms, practices, or objects. You may have such a feeling when you pick up a drum or rattle and begin to use it. Perhaps you tingle on hearing about the work that shamans do. Tingle phenomena also occur in nature and in conjunction with dreams, visions, and synchronicities.

At some point the interest, curiosity, and tingling become a strong call. The word *vocation* is appropriate here, for it feels like a calling to lead a religious or spiritual life or to be an alternative healer. Just as in shamanic cultures, the call is perceived at some point as coming from the spirit world.

You may hear the spirit call you in dreams at night or during meditation. You may hear its voice at odd moments during the day or night. The spirit may appear in the form of a deceased friend or relative; it may be an animal spirit that shows up in dreams or in waking life. The call can also come from the spirit of a divine being, saint, or angel in one of the mainstream religions. The calling will most likely become persistent, almost as if it will not leave you alone. And indeed, it will not, for the spirits are summoning you, inviting you to embark on a most serious path.

Life Crisis

The spirits may even use the classic life crisis to disrupt your routines, get your attention, and impress upon you the need to find healing and spiritual meaning in your life in shamanic ways. This is a traditional form of initiation in tribal societies, and it occurs in the Western world also. Some adult practitioners now recognize in earlier health crises, even childhood illnesses and accidents, the spiritual dimension of their misfortune that at the time was not clear to them or anyone else. The episode passed as just another crisis. But later in life the true significance of the event became clear. For many people, the crisis was a turning point in their lives, even though at the time they did not realize the shamanic implications of it.

The near-death experience (NDE) shares many similar elements with the shamanic journey, and it is a dramatic life crisis that can serve as a call to become a shaman. In an NDE the person feels released from the body and often finds himself or herself in a darkened tunnel or passageway with a bright, heavenly light at the end. There is an irresistible attraction to move toward the light. Somewhere along the way, the NDEer meets friends and relatives who have passed on; they approach to welcome the new arrival, but one of them or some higher spirit or voice announces that it is not the NDEer's time yet and the individual needs to return to earthly life. The NDEer does so, usually with utmost reluctance. After returning to the body, the person discovers he or she is in a hospital or medical center being treated for the cause of the near-death experience. When the individual recovers, he or she often has a newly formed sense of the meaning of life, the value of human existence, and dedicates his or her life to nobler goals.

Other life-changing crises in adult life may include the death of a loved one, the loss of a career, or a serious illness. Such events can lead people to rethink the meaning of life and come to a transformed sense of personal identity. These turning points can trigger a commitment to follow a more spiritual path through life because they are major blows to the ego and impress upon us our dependence upon higher powers. We come out of these crises with a humbler attitude about ourselves and a stronger sense of our need for divine assistance, which for the shaman often means the help of specific guardian spirits.

In all these life crises, whether major or minor, the person discovers that healing can take place only with help from the spirit world. The shamanic call is an opportunity, for the individual to meet his or her helping spirits.

FINDING A TEACHER

If any of the above circumstances have occurred in your life, and you feel called to learn and practice shamanism, how do you decide which variety of shamanism to pursue? In most cases, you may have no choice. The spirits will make it known, probably through a combination of life circumstances that lead you to a particular shamanic path. In other words, you will meet a shaman or teacher of shamanism and/or you will have visionary experiences, dreams, and synchronicities that make it clear whom you should study with or which tradition of shamanism is right for you.

Some people, however, discover that the shamanic tradition or practitioner that *initially* intrigues them proves to be incompatible with their lifestyle or the extent to which they are willing to change their lives. To study with traditional shamans may entail living near them, learning their language and customs, and adopting their belief systems, all of which may be too disruptive of your life and present commitments. Some other form of shamanism may be better suited for you, so you will proceed to explore other avenues.

But let's say that you are at a crossroads in your spiritual life and are trying to decide how to make an initial entry into the world of shamanism. How do you go about it? What should you bear in mind?

First, you'll find a vast array of shamanistic experiences available today. Workshops, seminars, retreats, training programs, pilgrimages to sacred sites, ongoing gatherings, and grassroots shamanic communities composed of people who are interested in and practice various forms of shamanism. Both native and non-native teachers offer instructional opportunities. Following are brief descriptions to distinguish among them:

A *workshop* is often a two-day or three-day gathering in which a leader teaches shamanic techniques so that people can take them home and incorporate them into their lives, either for healing purposes or as part of their spiritual practice.

A *seminar* is a teaching setting in which shamanism is discussed and possibly demonstrated, but more in the nature of an academic experience in which the participants' primary goal is to learn about shamanism but not how to practice it. Lectures, discussions, videos, and demonstrations usually make up a seminar.

A shamanic *retreat* may consist of a weekend of spiritual and healing activities with a shamanic focus. The intention of the shaman or retreat leader is to provide a setting in which participants can put aside their daily routines and come together, usually in a rural or pastoral setting, for spiritual renewal, inspiration, and healing. The goal here is not to present shamanism in any kind of academic way or teach specific techniques for further practice, but to provide a program of ritual and ceremony, meditation and reflection, song and dance for personal renewal.

A shamanic *training program* is more extensive than a workshop, seminar, or retreat, possibly lasting for several years with periodic gatherings that might be week-long or month-long. The goal is to train participants to be shamans or shamanic practitioners. On a traditional shamanic path, this might mean becoming an apprentice to an elder shaman and studying for many years. On a modern shamanic path, it means pursuing the complete course of programs offered by shamanic teachers and centers for shamanic studies.

Increasingly shamans and practitioners are offering *pilgrimage*s to sacred sites in various parts of the world, sometimes in conjunction with visits to indigenous shamans and with the opportunity to participate in their rituals and ceremonies. Some pilgrimages are more like tours for people interested in exploring ancient power places that have been honored by shamans and shamanic cultures and in conducting ceremonies, rituals, and other shamanic activities while there.

ONGOING PROGRAMS IN SHAMANISM

The renewed interest in shamanism has coincided with the founding of institutes and organizations to teach and promote shamanism. The following three organizations are representative of them.

Aloha International

Dr. Serge Kahili King founded Aloha International to teach the ancient shamanic wisdom of the Hawaiian and South Pacific islands. A shaman trained in Hawaiian and African traditions, King teaches the seven principles and corollaries of the traditional *huna* (hidden knowledge) philosophy of Hawaii. He calls his approach the Way of the Adventurer to stress the loving and cooperative nature of the universe. King's methods of shamanic training prepare men and women to be peacemakers in their daily lives. King says that they "know how to use the 'spirit of aloha' to work in a loving way with the forces of Nature and the powers of the mind to heal and enhance personal, social, and environmental relationships and events."

Like shamans everywhere, the Hawaiian shaman, or *kupua*, is effective because he or she knows how to work with the divine energy that pervades all created things. Called *mana* in Polynesia, this energy is found in greater concentrations in some objects, places, and people. Hawaiian shamans draw on this power, or what King calls "effective energy," to heal themselves and others, create beneficial realities, and influence natural events to enhance the underlying harmony and balance in the universe.

King's Huna Training, which includes workshops around the world and intensive sessions on the island of Kauai, teaches breathwork, telepathy, divination with stones, dream interpretation, shamanic journeying to other realities, and ways to cooperate with power animals and spirit guides. Shamanic bodywork includes traditional Hawaiian dance (hula) and light touch techniques used in conjunction with mental focus and feedback. King's program also trains teachers in *huna* and other aspects of shamanism and shamanic counseling. Aloha International sponsors ceremonies, rituals, and festivals in Hawaii and conducts pilgrimages to sacred sites in the islands.

The author of *Urban Shaman* and other books and articles on *huna* and Hawaiian shamanism, King challenges his students to bring shamanic healing to cities and metropolitan areas. "Anyone can be a shaman in the wilderness," he says. "What is really tough is being a shaman in the city...where we really need shamans." Pointing out that historically shamans have always been vital members of the societies in which they live, he calls upon modern practitioners of shamanism to bring their knowledge and practice to the problems of unhappiness and disharmony wherever they exist, in order to enrich human life and the health of the planet as a whole. "There is a kind of duty to the Earth," says King, "that the shaman can perform as no other."

Dance of the Deer Foundation Center for Shamanic Studies

Brant Secunda, a shaman in the Huichol tradition and founder of the Dance of the Deer Foundation Center for Shamanic Studies, located in California and southern France, is the adopted grandson of revered Huichol shaman don José Matsuwa, who passed into the next life at age 110 in 1990. Before he died, Matsuwa told Secunda, who had completed a twelve-year shaman's apprenticeship, "I leave you in my place. Tell your people to pray and follow the deer all the way to their hearts." The Dance of the Deer Foundation does just that, sponsoring workshops and pilgrimages around the world.

The Huichols number approximately 15,000 and are considered to be the last tribe in North America that has maintained its shamanic tradition and way of life since pre-Columbian times. Indeed, as with indigenous people everywhere, shamanic traditions pervade their entire lives, especially ceremony, mythology, artwork, not to mention planting corn and raising children.

Secunda invites people to join him at sacred sites to participate in Huichol ceremonial work. Pilgrimages are often to sacred mountains, such as Mt. Shasta and Mt. Rainier, and mountain ranges, such as the Smokies, the Catskills, and the Santa Cruz Mountains, all in the United States, as well as the mountains of Tuscany in Italy. Participants have rare opportunities to experience the spirit of place and develop a relationship with sacred landscapes through Huichol ceremony and shamanic activities. Dream sharing, vision quests, dancing the spirit of the deer (the animal most sacred to the Huichols), and meditations on the mysteries of Huichol yarn paintings are some of the experiences Secunda offers.

Secunda offers seminars and pilgrimages to places of power during the equinoxes and solstices for gatherings ranging in length from three to four days, as well as longer experiences of ten days to two weeks. For people who desire something more, Secunda also teaches ongoing in-depth study groups that meet three to four times a year for four years.

Secunda continues the healing work of Matsuwa, who taught that it was through prayer and sacred ceremony that we would reestablish the balance of life needed for the planet to survive. Said Matsuwa almost thirty years ago, "Unless we remember quickly what our lives are about, unless we celebrate through ceremony and prayer—our life source, the sun, and the sacred sea, the blessed land, the sky, and all things of nature—we will again face destruction."

The Foundation for Shamanic Studies

Unlike King and Secunda, who are preserving and transmitting shamanic traditions from specific indigenous cultures, Michael Harner is pioneering a unique approach to saving and spreading shamanic wisdom that has found receptive audiences worldwide, both among contemporary Westerners and some tribal people (such as the Inuit) who have lost shamanic practices after years of encroachment from Western civilization. Author of *The Way of the Shaman*, Harner calls this approach core shamanism.

As an anthropologist studying shamanism in South America, Harner was introduced to shamanic practices by the Jívaro people of the Amazon. Later, after returning to the United States and continuing to study and teach shamanism as an academic subject, Harner was intrigued by the similarities in shamanic techniques from radically different parts of the world, suggesting that shamanism arises out of basic human needs regardless of climate, culture, continent, or century. It is a human response to human problems. Following this line of thinking, Harner began teaching mainstream Americans the basic shamanic methods that were common to many shamanic traditions.

In the 1980s Harner created the Foundation for Shamanic Studies to continue this work. Currently based in California, the Foundation offers introductory and advanced training in core shamanism worldwide. It also sponsors ongoing training programs and expeditions to meet with indigenous shamans in their own lands, as well as inviting shamans to visit the United States and share shamanic knowledge and practices with Foundation students. The training programs include principles and methods for the shamanic journey, soul retrieval, extraction and healing, death and dying, the spirits of nature, divination, creativity, and shamanic counseling.

The Foundation's extensive international network of field associates and faculty on five continents help indigenous shamans to preserve or revive their traditions. The Foundation's Health Program works to introduce the value of shamanic healing methods to the mainstream medical community. An ongoing project to map nonordinary reality is creating a cross-cultural picture of the hidden universe explored and described by shamans throughout the ages.

After many years of teaching shamanism to average men and women, Harner has come to the conclusion that "people in general have shamanic abilities whether they are conscious of them or not." He says that it is important to activate this potential because shamanism can "foster a great respect for the universe, based on a feeling of oneness with all forms of life."

SHAMANIC DRUMMING CIRCLES AND NETWORKS

Among the more informal shamanic networks are the numerous drumming circles that spring up wherever practitioners seek support from like-minded individuals pursuing a shamanic path. Grassroots oriented, highly democratic, and nurturing, drumming circles tend to be small gatherings of people who meet to create sacred space in which to drum and journey. Most meet one or more times a month, usually in one member's home, and consist of anywhere from four or five to a dozen or more people. Some drumming circles will instruct newcomers in shamanic techniques used in their groups.

The format for the gathering varies, but in general the group sits in a circle around a lighted candle or simple altar-like arrangement in the center of the floor. Incense or herbs are burned to purify the space, the drums and rattles, and the members. The four directions are acknowledged by one member with a rattle, drum, invocation, or song. A few moments of reflective silence may be followed by a song or chant and then a discussion of what the session's journey should entail. A gathering may have time for two journeys: one with a common purpose for the entire group, the other for each individual to journey for a personal reason. Dancing to honor the members' power animals and helping spirits can be done to prepare for the journeys. Usually members share the content of their journeys with one another.

Some drumming circles are focused on healing work for the members, including divination and dream interpretation journeys. Sometimes the group will celebrate seasonal changes by honoring and journeying to the spirits of nature. Social and environmental causes also provide reasons for group journeying in the belief that individuals intervening in the spiritual realms can help causes and efforts that benefit society as a whole.

SHAMANISM ON-LINE

A growing number of people are sharing shamanic experiences and knowledge on the Internet. Chat rooms and Web sites are being created so that people around the world can connect to enhance their knowledge and practice of shamanism. In some cases, communities are forming, made up of individuals who know each other only through the Internet, sometimes only by their "spirit names." Shamanic artwork, songs, and journeys are shared; rituals are planned for later enactment. The field of techno-shamanism is still young and developing. Here are a few of the ways the Internet is being used:

- People decide on journey ideas, then journey, and get back on-line to share journeys.
- Some groups create icons or representations of their power animals and let them crawl onto the screen and sit in a circle to represent the meeting that would occur if participants were physically together.

- A person who needs healing can receive healing prayers, chants, or messages from others on-line.

Undoubtedly there will be increasingly surprising uses of the Internet for practitioners of shamanism as time goes on.

ETHICAL CONSIDERATIONS

The resurgence of interest in shamanism has raised ethical issues concerning adopting rites and customs from indigenous traditions and adapting them in settings and circumstances far removed from their cultures of origin. Cultural borrowing has been going on since the dawn of human history and is not likely to stop in our age of global communication and travel. Nor should we hope it stops, for no peoples want their culture to become frozen in time and unable to respond to the needs of the present era. And yet, for individuals who are concerned about honoring and respecting the ancient ways of our ancestors and the ancestors of other peoples, certain questions arise. Two of the most pressing are: When are we justified in adopting spiritual practices from other cultures? When are we justified in disregarding traditional taboos?

"Borrowing" from Native Traditions

Whichever path you follow, you should be aware of the dilemmas that can arise by the need to adopt or borrow native practices. There is considerable controversy about this, even within native communities. Some native shamans have lost face among their people for teaching traditional practices to non-natives, while others have been praised for doing so. Critics of this practice tend to see the situation as just another example of non-natives exploiting medicine people and native shamans and "stealing" their culture. Supporters see it in terms of gaining respect for indigenous spiritual and healing practices by teaching and sharing them with non-natives.

To complicate this matter, some native elders have trained non-natives as apprentices, even adopting them formally into their tribal communities. In a sense, they have passed the mantle on to Westerners, who then teach native shamanism to other non-natives. You should find out if a non-native teacher of a specific native tradition has been officially trained and commissioned to teach and conduct healing work in that tradition. Just having studied with native elders (taken workshops, for example) does not qualify one to teach native ways.

There are also shamanic practitioners who have not studied formally with native shamans but who learn traditional customs through reading or talks given by native shamans and then incorporate these practices into their own work. In deciding when such "borrowing" is appropriate, it is important to distinguish between practices that are universal and those that are specific to a particular culture. There is a lot of paraphernalia, ritual, ceremony, and practices involved in shamanism. It is difficult to know what is sacred and unique to a particular culture and what can be borrowed or adapted because it is found in many cultures worldwide, even in older European communities. These are often difficult judgment calls, and they will not produce universal agreement.

For example, sweat lodge practices are found worldwide. No culture or tribe has a monopoly on them. Many non-natives conduct sweat ceremonies. The problem arises when a non-native conducts a sweat following specific native procedures—for example, a Lakota sweat. Some sweat lodge leaders have been trained in "pouring water" by native elders with the intention of creating knowledgeable leaders who can perform this important ceremony for others. But some people conduct sweats along native lines without any training or blessing from elders.

Who is to say who can and who cannot pour water and according to which tradition? It is best to err on the side of respect and not take part in training sessions or ceremonies that you feel are being borrowed indiscriminately by practitioners who have not been properly trained and blessed in their work either by native elders or by shamanic practitioners who have been designated by native elders to train others.

Honoring Traditional Taboos

Respect for traditional ways can be difficult in areas concerning taboos. To what extent do modern practitioners of shamanism, even native shamans who are trying to adapt their customs to the contemporary world, have the right to change customs that are considered so sacred that they involve taboos? Typical taboos concern the time, place, and manner in which ritual and ceremonial activities can take place, such as where to perform a ritual, at what time of day or night to do certain ceremonies, when and how long to fast or abstain from sex, whether to allow visitors to watch or participate, when to separate men and women, and so forth.

The role of gender is an important issue in many traditional cultures. Most societies have some ceremonies that are restricted to either men or women. Then there are ceremonies open to both genders but in which men perform certain roles and women perform others. It is considered taboo to violate these time-honored traditions. To what extent can these customs be changed, and when should they be changed?

This is especially pertinent concerning women during their "moon time." Some male ceremonial leaders do not want women "on their moon" to sit in a circle, take part in a sweat, or handle sacred objects. In some cultures it would be inappropriate for a menstruating woman even to handle or prepare food at a feast after a ceremony. But there are some native elders who are challenging these taboos and changing them.

Many women and men are drawn to core shamanism precisely because it is free (or freer) from these traditional taboos. Since core shamanism consists of the basic generic practices found worldwide that can be engaged in without a specific cultural context, practitioners need not concern themselves with every ancient taboo found in those cultures. Core shamanism allows much more freedom for experimentation and adaptation of shamanic practices. Just as core shamanism is not dependent on specific religious beliefs, social customs, and ceremonial taboos, it can be flexible in terms of specific gender roles.

If the present trend continues, there will be a growing number of opportunities to learn shamanism. For one thing, the Earth itself is calling forth this ancient knowledge and practice that honors her and respects the spiritual dimensions of her many communities of life. People, too, are hungry for this Earth-honoring way of being in the world and relating to nature.

The three types of people doing shamanic work today—traditional shamans trained by the elders of their communities, Westerners trained by traditional shamans, and practitioners of core shamanism trained by a new type of elder emerging from the traditional practices found worldwide that transcend any particular culture—are all important figures in the shamanic renaissance, working to preserve and promote ancestral wisdom, the rich spiritual heritage that goes back to the earliest years of human existence. All are calling us to live more spiritually connected to the Earth and its many communities of life. All provide healing that encompasses body, mind, and soul. All remind us how important it is that we live in proper relationship to the greater universe.

As the Huichol shaman Matsuwa warns and encourages us:

> I see that many people here are so caught up in their own little lives that they are not getting their love up to the sun, out to the ocean, and into the earth…They forget the elements, forget the source of their life…You must study these things…Then one day, the Sea will give you heart; the Fire will give you heart; the Sun will give you heart.

The ongoing shamanic renaissance in its wide range of expressions and opportunities is offering all of us a chance to find a path with a heart.

Glossary:
The Language of Shamanism

Like any discipline, shamanism has a language of its own, special words that are part of the shamanic world view as well as specific meanings and uses for common words. The following glossary contains the words and phrases that occur most frequently in shamanic literature and practice. The definitions of these terms reflect the shamanic understanding of them and indicate how these words may be used in talking about shamanism.

Altered states of consciousness: Any state of consciousness different from the ordinary state of consciousness that we use in most daily activities. The shamanic state of consciousness is one of these. Others include: sleeping, dreaming, daydreaming, hypnotic states, inebriation, drug-induced states, and intense boredom. (See *ecstasy, trance, vision,* and *shamanic state of consciousness.*)

Amulet: An object used as a charm to bring good fortune or avert misfortune. Shamans may have amulets that represent specific spirits or personal powers. (See *power object, fetish,* and *talisman.*)

Ancestors/ancestral world: The deceased members of a community whose spirits continue to influence the living. Shamans respect the generations of people preceding the present generation and seek help or instruction from them because they represent the collective wisdom of their people.

Animals: In shamanism animals are seen as intelligent beings with whom humans share the planet and who provide food, clothing, tools, medicine, and companionship. Shamans also see animals as teachers of spiritual truths. (See *power animal* and *totem*.)

Animism: The belief that the natural world is alive, conscious, and spirit-filled. Shamans (as well as indigenous people in general) recognize and honor the individual spirits in all created things. A belief that the universe is filled with spirits does not preclude the belief in a Supreme Being who is the Creator of all.

Archetype: A fundamental, innate image in the unconscious that concentrates psychic or spiritual energy. Shamanic practitioners sometimes use the word to refer to the underlying power or psychic energy animating the images of the spirits they encounter in visionary states of consciousness.

Axis mundi: Literally, the "axis of the world," or the pole of the world. The sacred tree, pole, or mountain that a culture honors as the center of the universe and that connects the upper, middle, and lower worlds that constitute the shaman's cosmology. (See *world tree*.)

Click sticks: Sticks made out of hardwood that are struck together repeatedly to produce a mesmerizing sound. Some shamans use these in place of, or in addition to, drums or rattles.

Costumes: Sacred clothing worn by shamans for ceremonial or ritual purposes, often decorated with signs or symbols of the shaman's personal spirits or sources of power.

Wearing the costumes allows the shaman to shapeshift into—or to identify and merge with—the spirits depicted on the clothing. (See *masks* and *shapeshift*.)

Crystals: Wherever they are found, crystals are considered sacred stones that contain high concentrations of power, primarily because of their ability to concentrate and refract light. Shamans often use crystals as power objects.

Dance: Dance is used to honor the spirits, such as one's power animals or personal helping spirits. Ecstatic dancing is a method used by shamans to alter consciousness and merge with their helping spirits by letting the spirits move and dance through the body. (See *possession* and *shapeshift*.)

Disease/illness: The shaman sees disease or illness as a loss of spiritual power or life force. The shaman's general approach to healing involves extracting harmful energy that has entered the body and then restoring power by soul retrieval, power animal retrieval, or specific healing rituals to fill the patient with spiritual power and life force. (See *soul loss and soul retrieval*, *extraction*, and *mana*.)

Dismemberment: A process of spiritual empowerment and renewal in which helping spirits take the shaman's body apart; cleanse, purify, or doctor the pieces in some healing way; and put them back together again, often inserting the spiritual essence of other natural objects such as sacred stones, plants, or the basic elements. Dismemberment experiences occur in a shamanic state of consciousness, such as in dreams or during the shamanic journey.

Divination: Any method for discovering information about ordinary reality issues or problems through nonordinary methods, such as reading omens and signs, using special divinatory tools (e.g., runes, Tarot cards, the I Ching) or by asking the spirits directly for information. (See *omen* and *synchronicity*.)

Dreams: Shamans value dreams as opportunities for making contact with spirits and entering the spirit world while asleep. "Big" dreams about major life issues (as opposed to "little" dreams about mundane daily problems) contain vital information for the dreamer that may be contained in either literal or metaphorical language.

Drum: A widespread tool found in many cultures for calling spirits and entering the shamanic state of consciousness. Ritual drumming is not usually thought of as "music" in the sense of a rhythm or beat that accompanies a melody. Its purpose is ecstatic—that is, it alters the consciousness of those hearing it and mesmerizes them, freeing the mind and spirit from literal, linear thinking. In many cultures, drums must be made from certain types of wood and animal skins considered by the culture to be especially powerful or filled with spirit. The designated trees and animals are in some ways guardians of drum magic.

Drumming circle: A group of shamanic practitioners who meet together to drum, journey, and share visionary experiences on a regular basis. Such circles provide a community for practitioners that supports their shamanic work.

Ecstasy: Literally, "standing outside" oneself. A term that refers to the shaman's state of consciousness while in trance, during which the shaman's spirit or soul journeys into the spirit world or in some way makes contact with the spirits.

Extraction: A method of healing in which the shaman pulls or sucks from the patient's body the intrusion that is causing illness or disease. An intrusion may be thought of as the spiritual essence of a weakening or harmful condition that results when a person loses spiritual power or life force. (See *disease/illness.*)

Fetish: An object that embodies or is the habitation of a spirit or divine power and therefore deserves respect. Shamans use fetishes for protection, power, and healing. (See *amulet, talisman,* and *power object.*)

Guardians: Spirits that guard the thresholds into regions of the Otherworld. Also, spirits that guard and protect a shaman in both ordinary and nonordinary realities. Guardians may be the spirits of animals, the land, deities, angelic beings, or the deceased.

Initiation: A series of experiences that calls, trains, and prepares a person to become a shaman. Initiations are usually orchestrated by elder shamans and the neophyte shaman's spirit teachers. In many cases, the initial call from the spirits involves a life crisis, such as a serious illness, accident, or near-death experience. (See *near-death experience.*)

Journey: The shaman's experience of leaving ordinary reality and entering the nonordinary reality of the spirit realms while in an altered state of consciousness. The term usually refers to the shaman's intentional method of contacting the spirits by going to them, rather than a visitation by spirits in this reality. Unlike involuntary hallucinatory experiences that accompany certain mental disabilities, the shamanic journey is intentionally begun, involves a specific goal to be accomplished by the shaman, and is concluded by the shaman, who then returns to ordinary reality and his or her ordinary state of consciousness. (See *ordinary reality, nonordinary reality, upper world, middle world,* and *lower world.*)

Land of the dead: The region in the Otherworld where the souls of the deceased may dwell while awaiting rebirth or preparation for some higher state of existence. Often the spirits encountered there are confused or lost and have not arrived at the blissful, heavenly world that awaits them.

Lower world: The region of nonordinary reality that the shaman enters by going through an opening into the Earth, such as a cave, well, spring, tree root, or crack in a boulder. The realms of the Otherworld that exist beneath the surface of the Earth, as opposed to those above the sky or on the Earth. (See *journey, upper world,* and *middle world.*)

Magic: A term popularly used to mean the ability to make changes in ordinary reality through supernatural or psychic means. The word is appropriate to describe shamanic powers because most shamans develop keen psychic abilities, and by definition, a shaman is someone whose power and abilities come from helping spirits. (See *sorcery, witchcraft,* and *wizardry.*)

Mana: A Polynesian term meaning the life force or spiritual power that pervades the universe, often thought to be more potently concentrated in certain places, objects, foods, animals, and people. Similar to chi, manitou, wakanda, orenda, and other terms specific to particular cultures. (See *power*.)

Masks: A shaman wears masks that represent his or her animal spirits and other helping spirits. Masks are worn in ceremony and while dancing to facilitate the shaman's identification with those spirits and to merge with them in order to more fully acquire and utilize their helping powers. (See *costumes* and *shapeshift*.)

Medicine: An English word commonly used to refer to the spiritual power of Native American shamans and healers instead of the many indigenous terms for that power.

Medicine bundle: In some Native American traditions, the bag or pouch in which a medicine person carries sacred objects that contain or represent the spiritual powers he or she possesses. (See *power object*.)

Medicine person: The English phrase commonly used to refer to a man or woman who is a healer or spiritual facilitator among Native Americans.

Mediumship: The art and practice of calling upon helping spirits to enter ordinary reality and communicate or impart information from the spirit world. A *medium* is a person who uses trance states or other psychic abilities to connect with those spirits. (See *séance*.)

Middle world: The region between the upper and lower worlds, commonly seen as the reality in which we live our ordinary lives, but capable of being experienced in nonordinary states of consciousness in order to access the spirit forces present here. (See *journey*, *lower world*, and *upper world*.)

Near-death experience (NDE): Technically, that which occurs when the vital functions of the mind and body cease temporarily. Sometimes a person who has a near-death experience recognizes it as a call from the spirits to pursue the training and life of a shaman. There are similarities also between the classic elements of the shamanic journey and the elements of a near-death experience, such as losing awareness of the immediate surroundings, feeling that one is leaving the physical body, passing through a tunnel, encountering a lighted area beyond the tunnel, and meeting welcoming spirits. (See *initiation*.)

Necromancy: The practice of contacting the spirits of the deceased for instruction and information concerning current life problems. (See *séance* and *medium*.)

Nonordinary reality: A phrase coined by Carlos Castañeda to refer to the experiences that occur in altered states of consciousness such as dreams and trance. It can also mean the Otherworld; the spirit realms; the "place" outside of time and space that the shaman encounters in visionary states of consciousness, such as during the shamanic journey. The phrase is used to emphasize that what is perceived in dreams and visions is real, but partakes of a different kind of reality from what is perceived in ordinary states of consciousness. (See *ordinary reality* and *journey*.)

Omen: A sign, condition, or event that carries meaning or information about something apparently unrelated to it but which a person who knows how to read such signs can understand. A shaman's skill in recognizing and reading omens is analogous to the ability to find meaning and information in nonordinary sources and in nonordinary states of consciousness. (See *divination*, *second sight*, and *synchronicity*.)

Ordinary reality: The counterpart of Carlos Castañeda's *nonordinary reality*. The phrase refers to this world; the physical-material realms; things and events that exist in time and space as they are perceived and understood in a normal waking state of consciousness. (See *nonordinary reality*.)

Otherworld: A word that can mean any or all of the regions of the spirit world or the normally invisible/inaudible realms of spiritual power. Nonordinary reality; the place outside of time and space; the faery realms. In general, the place where shamans journey in ecstatic states of consciousness. (See *nonordinary reality*.)

Out-of-the-body experience: The experience of one's soul or spirit temporarily leaving the body, usually in an altered state of consciousness, and traveling to other places usually in this reality (the middle world). Unlike the shamanic journey, in which the shaman's traveling spirit enters the spirits' world and/or sees and hears the "spirit shapes of things" (to use Black Elk's phrase), an out-of-the-body experience usually transports the individual to some place in ordinary, physical reality where the person sees and hears events occurring in ordinary reality at that moment. (See *journey* and *soul flight*.)

Possession: The condition in which another spirit, such as a power animal or deity, enters the shaman's consciousness and body in order to give the shaman power, understanding, or abilities that he or she would not have alone or in a less intimate connection with that spirit. Spirit possession is often accompanied by ecstatic dancing and chanting. (See *shapeshift*.)

Power: From a shamanic point of view, spiritual or psychic power that comes from the shaman's intimate relationship with helping spirits or nature. Often equated with the life force or divine energy that permeates the universe. Certain places, objects, and people contain more power or greater concentrations of power than others. (See *mana*.)

Power animal: A shaman's helping spirit that has the form of a specific kind of animal. An animal spirit that instructs, guides, guards, and accompanies a shaman in visionary work. The word *power* does not, in this sense, refer to the physical size or strength of the animal, but to the animal's ability to help the shaman spiritually. (See *totem*.)

Power object: An object, such as a stone, shell, feather, mirror, knife, or bone, that is invested with spiritual meaning and significance for the shaman. An object used in healing and ritual activities to focus the shaman's attention and impart spiritual power to the work. (See *amulet*, *talisman*, and *fetish*.)

Power song: A song, often taught by the spirits, that a shaman sings as part of spiritual and healing work. A song that increases the shaman's sense of power or connection with the spirits. A song to honor the spirits.

Power spot: A place in nature where the shaman experiences the Otherworld more intensely, where certain spirits dwell, or where the Earth energies are exceptionally evident. A place a shaman may use as a personal retreat or for ritual work. (See *sacred site*.)

Prayer: Usually a verbal expression of one's relationship to the spirits, a call to the spirit world for help, or a statement of gratitude for spiritual help.

Psychoactive/psychotropic substances: Food, drink, plants, or herbs that alter one's usual perceptions of reality. Psychoactive plants are often used in indigenous cultures by highly trained shamans to facilitate visionary experiences in themselves or others.

Psychopomp: Literally, a "leader of souls." Shamans are psychopomps when they lead or conduct the soul of a dying person into the next world or assist at births to help the new soul make a safe entrance into this life. A standard service performed by shamans in many cultures.

Rattle: An instrument that produces clattering sounds when shaken, used by shamans for ceremonial purposes, to call the spirits, or to focus and alter consciousness for visionary activities.

Sacred site: A place revered by shamans because it is a power spot, a dwelling place for certain spirits, a place where ceremonial activity occurs, or a site where important events transpired in the history of the tribe or in the shaman's personal life. (See *power spot*.)

Sacrifice: Literally, "to make holy or sacred." A sacred offering or gift to the spirits in gratitude or in petition, or the act of offering the gift. A sacrificial object is usually valuable or precious to the person who offers it. Shamans make sacrifices to the spirits in appreciation for their assistance or to seek their assistance.

Séance: A session or an activity in which a person, called a medium, uses a trance or ecstatic state to make contact with spirits. Shamans sometimes function as mediums during their work by calling spirits to speak through them. (See *mediumship*.)

Second sight: Sometimes called simply "the Sight." The ability to see beyond the physical realms or to perceive with interior senses things that are normally invisible, such as the spirit world, concealed conditions, the past or future, events occurring at a distance, or the significance of signs and omens. (See *omen*.)

Shaman: A healer whose power and knowledge derive from intimate, ongoing relationships with personal helping spirits. Contact with helping spirits occurs primarily, although not solely, in altered states of consciousness in which the shaman journeys into the spirit realms for instruction and personal empowerment.

Shamanic practitioner: Any person who practices shamanism, but usually referring to someone who has not been trained within a traditional indigenous society. A person in the mainstream culture who has been trained in shamanic methods and techniques and uses them in ways similar to shamans, but with more freedom for innovation and eclecticism. A person who uses shamanism as a spiritual practice.

Shamanic state of consciousness: A phrase coined by Michael Harner to refer to the altered state of consciousness typical of a shaman while journeying into the spirit world. A state of consciousness similar to a waking dream, induced by closing the eyes, relaxing, and listening to some form of sonic driving, such as a drumbeat or the sound of a rattle. (See *trance, vision, sonic driving*, and *Otherworld*.)

Shamanism: The beliefs and practices originating in hunting-gathering-fishing cultures that deal with developing and maintaining ongoing relationships with the spirits of nature, elements, ancestors, and other divine beings. A system of healing and personal instruction based on partnerships with helping spirits. The practice of journeying to the spirit world for instruction and power. (See *shaman* and *shamanic practitioner*.)

Shapeshift: The act of altering consciousness in order to merge or become one with the consciousness of some particular animal, plant, or object. A shaman shapeshifts by allowing the spirit of another entity to merge with his or her own in order to experience the power and wisdom of that entity, such as a power animal or element. In a shapeshifted state, a shaman might be seen by others as exhibiting the aura or even the physical appearance of the entity. (See *possession*.)

Skeletal art: Depictions of the skeletal structure of the human body found in Paleolithic rock and cave art and also on the drums, shields, and clothing of shamans. Bones are the most indelible part of the human body, surviving long after death, and serve as reminders of the continued existence of the human spirit in the next world.

Smudging: Ritual cleansing or purifying by wafting over the body or the object to be cleansed the smoke from sacred herbs, such as sage, cedar, and sweetgrass.

Sonic driving: A constant, monotonous, mesmerizing sound, such as that from a drum, rattle, or click sticks, used by shamans to induce an altered state of consciousness.

Sorcery: The art or ability to derive and use power or knowledge from the spirit world. Early accounts of shamanism written by European travelers and explorers refer to shamans as sorcerers. (See *witchcraft* and *wizardry*.)

Soul flight: Also known as spirit flight. A phrase referring to the shamanic journey, in which the shaman's soul, spirit, or consciousness leaves ordinary reality and moves into the nonordinary realms of the spirit world. (See *out-of-the-body experience* and *journey*.)

Soul loss and soul retrieval: In shamanic terms, disease, illness, and misfortune can occur when a person loses soul or parts of the soul—that is, a part of the person's vital essence or life force. Soul can leave during traumatic experiences, such as the death of a loved one, abuse, war, or a near-death experience. Soul can also be stolen intentionally or unintentionally by another person. Shamans in many cultures perform soul retrieval journeys and rituals to restore the soul or vital essence to a person suffering from its loss.

Spirits: Conscious, intelligent, communicative beings, normally imperceptible to the human senses, who dwell in certain places and objects in ordinary reality or in the nonordinary realms of the Otherworld. Types of spirits include the spirits of nature (the elements and the land), animal spirits, the deceased, angels, deities, and any other noncorporeal entities that shamans encounter in a shamanic state of consciousness. Shamans have ongoing, personal relationships with various spirits who instruct them on the nature of the universe and ways to serve the human community.

Spirit keeper: A spirit in charge of a certain place, such as a mountain or valley, or the spirit in charge of an important activity, such as healing, hunting, giving birth, etc. (See *spirits*.)

Sweat lodge: A small hut to which heated stones are brought or where special fires are built for the purpose of ritual cleansing or purification. The discomfort caused by the heat is conducive to intense spiritual and visionary experiences that can facilitate healing, prayer, and the honoring of spirits. Many indigenous cultures have some form of sweat lodge tradition that is an important practice for shamans as well as others in the community.

Synchronicity: A term coined by psychologist Carl Jung to refer to the occurrence of two apparently unrelated events which, together, have profound significance for the person observing them. A synchronicity alerts the observer to the interconnection between interior states of consciousness and exterior conditions in the physical world. Shamans strongly believe in these connections between the inner and outer life and view synchronicities as evidence of spirit activity. (See *omen* and *web of life*.)

Taboo: An object, place, person, or activity that is considered sacred or powerful in some way and consequently around which there are certain prohibitions and requirements. Shamanic world views incorporate various taboos to acknowledge, honor, and respect the spirit and consciousness in various created things.

Talisman: An object, like an amulet, used for protection or power. It is usually engraved, carved, or decorated for some specific purpose. (See *amulet, fetish,* and *power object.*)

Totem: An animal or plant, or a type of animal or plant, that is considered an ancestor or special guardian. All the members of a tribe or clan may have the same animal or plant totem and thus be related to one another and to the totem. A totem animal is not necessarily a shaman's power animal. (See *power animal.*)

Trance: A state of consciousness in which a person is not as aware of the ordinary world as when fully awake and alert. Consequently, the attention can be turned to nonordinary realities that are usually imperceptible in ordinary states of consciousness. There are various levels of trance, from slight daydreaming to a coma-like condition. Shamans use trance-like states when doing visionary work, such as journeying, healing, dancing, and communicating with spirits. (See *shamanic state of consciousness, ecstasy, ordinary reality,* and *nonordinary reality.*)

Trickster: The deity, animal, or spirit who fools, amuses, interferes, challenges, and upsets normal activity. Usually a scoundrel but a likable individual who is responsible for certain cultural gifts, such as corn, fire, sexuality, and law, but who operates outside the normal rules of society. In some cultures, coyote, raven, hare, and fox are tricksters.

Upper world: The region of nonordinary reality that a shaman enters by going through a hole, crack, or opening in the sky. The spirit realms that exist on the other side of the sky, as opposed to those in the middle and lower worlds. (See *journey*, *lower world*, and *middle world*.)

Vision: A term referring to what is experienced in a dream-like state of consciousness, such as during a shamanic journey, while chanting or dancing, or in night dreams. Visionary knowledge and experiences often involve visual imagery but are not restricted to it. Hearing and sensing while in other states of consciousness are equally valid channels of visionary experiences.

Vision quest: An intentional excursion into the natural world for an extended period of silence, solitude, fasting, prayer, and other austerities for the purpose of communicating with spirits and receiving a vision or a deeper understanding of the meaning of one's life and/or the universe. Most spiritual paths have some form of vision quest, and shamans in all cultures use it for empowerment.

Web of life: A phrase that refers to the interconnectedness of all created things. Shamans have a strong belief in the web of life, engendered by their experiences in the spirit world and in their healing practices.

Witchcraft: The spiritual-magical-psychic powers and practices of a woman or man who, usually but not always, lives and operates on the fringe of society or outside the dominant religious/political power structure. Witchcraft tends to include the same healing and spiritual services for the community as those offered by shamans in their cultures. In fact, many elements of European witchcraft are the vestiges of older shamanic traditions. Many early accounts of shamans by European travelers refer to them as witches. (See *wizardry* and *sorcery*.)

Wizardry: Powers and practices considered to be beyond normal human abilities and therefore derived from the spirits. Early descriptions of male shamans by European travelers and explorers frequently refer to them as wizards. (See *sorcery* and *witchcraft*.)

World tree: A culture's sacred tree that is considered to be the axis mundi, or center of the universe. A classic shamanic symbol of the connections in the three-part universe of upper, middle, and lower worlds. (See *axis mundi*.)

Sources

Bennett, Hal Zina, "From the Heart of the Andes: An Interview with Q'ero Shaman Americo Yabar," *Shaman's Drum* (Fall 1994).

Boyd, Doug, *Rolling Thunder* (New York: Dell Publishing, 1974),.

Buckley, Daniel, "The Story Teller," Tucson Citizen, June 25, 1990, 3B.

Campbell, Joseph, *The Flight of the Wild Gander* (Chicago: Regnery Gateway, 1969).

Carmichael, Alexander , *Carmina Gadelica: Hymns and Incantations* (Hudson, NY: Lindisfarne Press, 1992).

Castañeda, Carlos, *Journey to Ixtlan* (New York: Simon and Schuster, 1972).

Cowan, Eliot, "Interview with an Irish Shaman," *Shamanism: Quarterly of The Foundation for Shamanic Studies* (Summer 1992, vol. 5, no. 1).

Cowan,Eliot, *Plant Spirit Medicine* (Newberg, OR: Swan-Raven & Company, 1995).

Drury, Nevill, *The Elements of Shamanism* (Rockport, MA: Element Books, 1991).

Goldman, Caren, "The Garden of Lost Souls," *Yoga Journal* (September/October 1994).

Halifax, Joan, *Shamanic Voices: A Survey of Visionary Narratives* (New York: E. P. Dutton, 1979).

Halifax, *Shamanic Voices*.

Harner, Michael, "The Ancient Wisdom in Shamanic Culture," *Shamanism*, comp. by Shirley Nicholson (Wheaton, IL: The Theosophical Publishing House, 1987).

Harner, Michael, *The Way of the Shaman* (New York: Bantam Books.

Hawaiian Shaman Training pamphlet, published by Aloha International, P.O. Box 665, Kilauea, HI 96754.

Heart, Bear and Larkin, Molly , "In the Footsteps of My Teachers: Lessons with Little Beaver and Old Seer," in *Shaman's Drum* (Spring 1996).

Kalweit, Holger, *Dreamtime & Inner Space: The World of the Shaman* (Boston: Shambhala, 1988).

Kalweit, *Dreamtime & Inner Space.*

King, Serge, "The Way of the Adventurer," *The American Theosophist* (Fall 1985).

Lame Deer, John (Fire) and Erdoes, Richard, *Lame Deer: Seeker of Visions* (New York: Simon & Schuster, 1972).

Margolin, Malcolm, *The Way We Lived: California Indian Stories, Songs & Reminiscences* (Berkeley: Heyday Books, 1993).

Neihardt, John G., *Black Elk Speaks* (New York: Simon & Schuster, 1975).

Pamphlet published by the Dance of the Deer Foundation, P.O. Box 699, Soquel, CA 95073.

Peters, Larry G., "China Expedition 1995: A Personal Account," *Shamanism: Quarterly The Foundation for Shamanic Studies* (Spring/Summer 1996, vol. 9, no. 1).

Somé, Malidoma Patrice, *Of Water and the Spirit: Ritual, Magic, and Initiation in the Life of an African Shaman* (New York: Penguin Books, 1994).

Somé, *Of Water and Spirit,*177–78.

White, Timothy, "Northwest Coast Medicine Teachings: An Interview with Johnny Moses," *Shaman's Drum* (Spring 1991).

Bibliography

Cowan, Eliot. *Plant Spirit Medicine*. Newberg, OR: Swan-Raven & Company, 1995.

Cowan, Tom. *Shamanism as a Spiritual Practice for Daily Life*. Freedom, CA: The Crossing Press, 1996.

Eliade, Mircea. *Shamanism: Archaic Techniques of Ecstasy*. Princeton, NJ: Princeton University Press, 1974.

Halifax, Joan. *Shamanic Voices: A Survey of Visionary Narratives*. New York: E. P. Dutton, 1979.

Harner, Michael. *The Way of the Shaman*. San Francisco: Harper & Row, 1990.

Ingerman, Sandra. *Soul Retrieval: Mending the Fragmented Self*. San Francisco: Harper Collins, 1991.

Johnson, Kenneth. *North Star Road: Shamanism, Witchcraft & the Otherworld Journey*. St. Paul, MN: Llewellyn Publications, 1996.

Kalweit, Holger. *Dreamtime & Inner Space: The World of the Shaman*. Boston: Shambhala, 1988.

King, Serge Kahili. *Urban Shaman*. New York: Simon & Schuster, 1990.

Somé, Malidoma Patrice. *Of Water and the Spirit: Ritual, Magic, and Initiation in the Life of an African Shaman*. New York: Penguin, 1994.

Walsh, Roger. *The Spirit of Shamanism*. Los Angeles: Jeremy P. Tarcher, 1990.

Other Titles in the Same Series
by Book Faith India

For catalog & more information, write to:
PILGRIMS BOOK HOUSE
P. O. Box 3872, Thamel
Kathmandu, Nepal
Tel : 977-1-424942, 425919
Fax : 977-1-424943
E-mail : pilgrims@wlink.com.np
Website : www.pilgrimsbooks.com